JEET KUNE DO
THE ARSENAL OF SELF-EXPRESSION

FOREWORD BY TED WONG

Teri Tom

TUTTLE PUBLISHING
Tokyo • Rutland, Vermont • Singapore

Please note that the publisher and author of this instructional book are NOT RESPONSIBLE in any manner whatsoever for any injury that may result from practicing the techniques and/or following the instructions given within. Martial arts training can be dangerous—both to you and to others—if not practiced safely. If you're in doubt as to how to proceed or whether your practice is safe, consult with a trained martial arts teacher before beginning. Since the physical activities described herein may be too strenuous in nature for some readers, it is also essential that a physician be consulted prior to training.

Published by Tuttle Publishing, an imprint of Periplus Editions (HK) Ltd., with editorial offices at 364 Innovation Drive, North Clarendon, Vermont 05759 U.S.A.

Library of Congress Cataloging-in-Publication Data

Tom, Teri.
  Jeet kune do : the arsenal of self-expression / Teri Tom.
     p. cm.
  Includes bibliographical references and index.
  ISBN 978-0-8048-3932-7 (pbk. : alk. paper)
  1. Jeet Kune Do. I. Title.
  GV1114.6.T64 2009
  796.8--dc22
                                    2009006291

ISBN-13: 978-0-8048-3932-7

Distributed by

North America, Latin America & Europe
Tuttle Publishing
364 Innovation Drive
North Clarendon, VT 05759-9436 U.S.A.
Tel: 1 (802) 773-8930; Fax: 1 (802) 773-6993
info@tuttlepublishing.com
www.tuttlepublishing.com

Japan
Tuttle Publishing
Yaekari Building, 3rd Floor
5-4-12 Osaki
Shinagawa-ku
Tokyo 141 0032
Tel: (81) 3 5437-0171; Fax: (81) 3 5437-0755
tuttle-sales@gol.com

Asia Pacific
Berkeley Books Pte. Ltd.
61 Tai Seng Avenue #02-12
Singapore 534167
Tel: (65) 6280-1330; Fax: (65) 6280-6290
inquiries@periplus.com.sg
www.periplus.com

First edition
13 12 11 10 09   5 4 3 2 1

Printed in Singapore

TUTTLE PUBLISHING® is a registered trademark of Tuttle Publishing, a division of Periplus Editions (HK) Ltd.

CONTENTS

FOREWORD BY TED WONG

"True refinement seeks simplicity." —Bruce Lee

At different times and in different places there suddenly appear individuals who produce something completely new in their chosen fields. Whether in science or art or sports, they have the confidence to go beyond the known and predictable, to arrive at something entirely different from what went before. Bruce Lee, in his short life, boldly pursued one thing, an original martial art. What he developed was a revolutionary style of unarmed combat, and it was an art only, and immediately, original to him: not a derivation, not a combination, not a collaboration.

To Bruce Lee there was a profound difference between his JKD, and all other martial art disciplines. The fixed nature of traditional martial arts was, he thought, unworkable—methods too busy, too complex, and too rigid to be strong. He did not want superficial strength. The strength he wanted would come from a scientific approach to gravity and weight, efficiency and balance, force and speed. Driven to create a singular style, Lee placed the full-control of what he was forming in the hands of the only person he completely trusted—himself. He drew on his own character—his instincts, his physical conditioning, and his forceful intellect to communicate the distinctiveness of his art. Refined mechanics, exacting execution, incredible power—this is JKD.

Only one individual, Bruce Lee, truly created and shaped JKD, and only Lee completely brought it to life from his personal conviction, determination and vision. But nothing comes from nothing—there is always something that precedes. Lee did have inspirations. They were not, however, of Eastern origin, but Western fighters: boxers Jack Dempsey and Jim Driscoll, and the fencer Aldo Nadi. Studying them reinforced Lee's definition of his own method. He made JKD basic principles few in number, but adaptable and dependable under any situation. Less being more, Lee emphasized disciplined, simplified positioning and movement, supported by effective analysis of diverse circumstance.

Embodied by Bruce Lee in his lifetime, the truth of his art is clearly evident in Lee's films, his interviews, and especially in his writings. It is outrageous, then, to suggest that JKD is an extension of another discipline—a suggestion that runs completely counter to his life and work. And it is insulting to see JKD deemed by some as obsolete or so weak that it requires additional techniques to sustain it—a characterization which subverts Lee's significant form of unarmed combat. Let me state this plainly: no student of Lee's has surpassed him; no one knew better than Lee what he was doing and why; no one is qualified to alter Lee's work. Bruce Lee created JKD. Add something to it, or take something away, and you are doing something other than what Lee taught.

I first met Bruce Lee in 1967 at his school in Los Angeles' Chinatown. Even before our meeting, however, I knew him from television, in his role as Kato on The Green Hornet. Lee's Kato was like a cat—quick, graceful and powerful. His appeal far outshone that of the show's hero. Never had an Asian character been portrayed in Western popular culture like Lee portrayed Kato—tough, cool, confident. It was the beginning of Lee's iconic celebrity as the first Asian superstar. It is easy now to forget how unique Lee was. Martial artists are everywhere in the popular culture today, but forty years ago there was only one: Bruce Lee. Even with Asian stars such as Jet Li, Steven Chow and Jackie Chan, and with incredible advances in special effects, which allow anyone to look physically amazing on film—Bruce Lee remains without peer. His image and style still resonate with compelling effectiveness.

The first time Bruce Lee ever spoke to me, in our second class, it was to demand: "WHO ARE YOU?" There had been a mix-up with my registration. After I explained, we started to talk in Chinese, and found that our similar upbringings had given us things in common. Yet standing next to Lee, there was no similarity between us whatsoever. I was a skinny,

reserved young man. I had no martial arts training, but was instead a kind of blank page, which, perhaps, was my biggest asset. Like a "mad scientist" with an experiment, Lee could mold my understanding, and completely shape my experience. The first thing he did was to have me buy weights and start on a regimen to develop physically. Then within a short time, I began private lessons at his home.

Going to classes at his school, and then, privately training, gave me a unique opportunity to observe the formation of Lee's art. The school's classes were practical and formulaic, devised around a curriculum of modified Chinese kung fu, necessary to impart discipline on a large group. But the class bore no similarity to Lee's private lessons. There, Lee was in a different zone, teaching a kind of free form, experimental course in his developing art. Increasingly, he was content to instruct privately. Seeing the school's curriculum as outmoded and unrelated to his work, he closed the school. He did not care about establishing a commercial venture, but instead, turned towards achieving a discipline.

In private instruction, Lee completely oversaw the dissemination of his theories and techniques. Some students received different levels of instruction than others, different degrees of what he knew. Evolving rapidly, he demanded precision from himself and expected students to follow without argument. He explained little, and had scant patience for repeating what he demonstrated. If you didn't get it quickly, then you were out. As he expanded his techniques, Lee kept most of the mechanics in his head, always reserving something for himself—a knowledge that made him the "master of the art." He was not about to impart "the keys to the kingdom" without their being justly earned.

Lee's mechanics were as much rooted in the intellectual as the physical. To fight like Bruce Lee, one had to learn to think like Lee. I was one of very few people taught by him directly—training, sparring, and "hanging out" for seven years. By listening closely and watching attentively, I began to be aware of the underlying precepts of JKD. For 15 years after Lee's death, I continued to study the structure of his form. And for 15 years after that, as I implemented what I learned, I discovered even more. JKD consists of few techniques and is without a lot of show or flash. Kicks and punches are concise, defined with form following function. During his life, I admired Bruce Lee and deeply appreciated the skills that he taught me. Since his death, I have honored him. Every lesson I teach, I ask myself, "Would he approve?" With every problem I encounter, I ask, "how would he approach this situation?"
I deeply regret that at the time of Bruce Lee's death all his students did not come together to pool knowledge and form a united front to continue his work. Sharing, discussing, perhaps arguing, we might have arrived at some common ground to go forward, and attempt to systematize JKD at that time. The force of Lee's personality had connected us when he was alive, but when he died, we all went our separate ways. Since then, I have seen wildly inaccurate interpretations of JKD. Some stray from and others even contradict Lee's intentions. It pains me to see his legacy undermined by perspectives skewed or self-serving. Never, in the time I knew him, did I see him collaborate with anyone, nor did I see him base his work on elements from other martial arts. Today, there are all sorts of schools and all sorts of instructors who claim to be teaching Bruce Lee's method—there is nothing in them that I recognize as his.

I hold fast to what I learned; I vividly remember Lee's words and actions. Though I have never advertised, or had a school, I have been a private instructor for more than thirty years. Individuals from different countries and backgrounds have sought me out for instruction because of my direct line to Bruce Lee, and I have shown them the essence of what I was personally taught by him.

As I was Lee's devoted student, so I consider Teri Tom my student—my top student. For over ten years, she has spent more time learning, discussing and investigating the fundamentals of Lee's art with me than any student with whom I have worked. Her attentiveness in developing the discipline accurately, and her devotion in seeing it raised to the level that Bruce Lee envisioned in his life, heartens my belief that through her, the art I learned and teach will be passed on to future generations.

It is tragic that the art that defined Lee—one he nurtured, guarded, and methodically shaped and executed—continues to be misunderstood by so many. It is my deepest hope that Lee's art, as he taught it, will once again, with Teri Tom's excellent new book, be studied and appreciated. She has explored Bruce Lee's writings and examined the sources of his inspiration. Here she offers an impeccably researched, thorough and realistic presentation of Lee's art and its application insuring that the discipline he developed in his short life, will not perish from misguided egos, insincere motives, or plain stupidity. By placing Lee's art in proper perspective, Tom challenges all the absurdities being espoused in his name. I believe Lee would see in her, as I do, an intelligence, resolve and courage similar to his own. Plainly stated what Bruce Lee taught and practiced is contained in this book.

—Ted Wong, November 2008

AUTHOR'S NOTE

Photo by Rick Hustead

As you may already know, the volume that you now hold in your hands was preceded several years ago by a little book called *The Straight Lead: The Core of Bruce Lee's Jun Fan Jeet Kune Do®*. Through the study of a single technique, I traced the evolution of Bruce Lee's martial arts development out of Western boxing and fencing. I thought it important to come right out of the gate with an argument for the technique that is really the cornerstone of Jeet Kune Do, or more precisely in Bruce Lee's own words, "the core of Jeet Kune Do." All other aspects of the art—other punches, evasive techniques, even the stance—were selected and developed around delivery of the straight lead.

While we briefly cover the lead punch in this book, we don't have enough room here to go into its history and origins. Nor do we have the space to cover some of the finer details of the mechanics. For a full understanding of the art, then, I recommend your reading this book's predecessor, as the material you are about to read is a natural progression from *The Straight Lead*. I've taken some of the basic mechanics and strategies covered in that book and applied them to the rest of the JKD arsenal.

The purpose of both volumes is to fill in some of the instructional gaps between the *Fighting Method* series and the *Tao of Jeet Kune Do*. As we noted in the last book, Bruce Lee did not intend for the *Tao* to be published as an instruction manual. It is merely a collection of his personal notes, most of which were taken from other sources. It is not a how-to book—nor is the *Fighting Method* series. Unfortunately, Bruce Lee was never able to assemble what became the *Fighting Method* series as an instructional manual, and much of the material had become outdated by the time of his death. The photos that would comprise the *Fighting Method* books were taken early in the development of JKD in 1967. If you compare them to movie stills from *Game of Death* in 1972 and *Enter the Dragon* in 1973, you'll see that he'd made some very important modifications in the interim.

This is where we are so fortunate to have Ted Wong's powers of observation and analysis. As I've mentioned elsewhere, Ted Wong spent more time in private instruction with Bruce Lee than any of Lee's other students. Unlike many who claim to know Bruce Lee's art, Wong may be the only one truly qualified to make that claim. He was there. This is on record in Bruce Lee's own Day-Timer® notes.[1,2] Even more important than the frequency of sessions, though, is the time of those sessions. Wong had the fortune to study privately with Bruce Lee more than anyone else, but he also did so during the last stages of JKD development, right up until Lee's death in 1973. He is the most frequent, if not the only—and this is documented as such in Lee's own handwriting—witness to JKD in its most advanced stages. Without his tireless study, Bruce Lee's life's work would be lost forever.

What you will find in the following pages are a lot of the small details that Ted Wong had observed during his time with Bruce Lee and his own discoveries as to *how* and *why* they work. You might think of this book as providing the information that connects the dots found in the *Tao*. Those small, nuanced movements—like footwork, feinting, weight transfer, and the sequencing of those elements—and how they're used to transition from movement to movement make all the difference. But they are not discussed in the *Fighting Method* series, which for the most part, just catalogs the techniques of JKD. Nor are they illustrated in the *Tao*. This book should be considered a supplement to both.

I've argued many times that Bruce Lee was and still is light years ahead of his time. In most sports, it's now a given that coaches incorporate principles of biomechanics into their training. For some reason, this shift has not occurred to the same degree in the martial arts. Lee, however, was already looking into biomechanics in the 1960's, when it was still unconventional to do so. As you'll see, there are passages in the *Tao* taken directly from one of the first kinesiology textbooks, which was written by Philip J. Rasch and R.K. Burke. You'll find that all the techniques in the JKD arsenal are in accordance with the principles of biomechanics and kinesiology and still hold true and are taught today. Because this is such an important part of JKD, I've dedicated a chapter solely to general biomechanics. As we go through each technique, you will want to refer to this chapter for further insight on the how's and why's behind them.

Finally, there has been so much malicious misrepresentation of Bruce Lee's art over the last three decades, I've cross-referenced, as I did in my last book, the original sources of Bruce Lee's writings. In accordance with the saying "talent borrows, genius steals," almost all of the technical notes that comprise the *Tao of Jeet Kune Do* and *Commentaries on the Martial Way* are passages that come from other sources. You will see that there are no references to wing chun, kali, or escrima. There is also very little coverage of grappling techniques. This is why there are only nine pages of grappling techniques in the *Tao*. The majority of that book, as is the case with Bruce Lee's personal notes, is almost exclusively comprised of passages on boxing technique and fencing strategy. Having actually been through Bruce Lee's handwritten notebooks, I can say that, with the exception of the sections on Zen philosophy, virtually everything is Western in origin. Most of the fencing notes come from Aldo Nadi, Julio Martinez Castello, and Roger Crosnier. There are also boxing influences from a wide range of sources including Jack Dempsy, Jim Driscoll, Thomas Inch, Edwin Haislet, Peter McInnes, and Bobby Neill.

The passages in those volumes of personal notes make up the majority of the *Tao* and are also found in *Commentaries on the Martial Way*. These notes are from the most advanced stages of JKD development. There are those who claim all sorts of origins of JKD—from Filipino martial arts to wing chun. They will want to argue this point endlessly. I suggest they first take the cross-references here, track down the original sources and see for themselves, clear as daylight, that Jeet Kune Do is *Western* in origin.

THE NECESSITY OF TECHNIQUE

Before we get into the nitty gritty of technical explanations, a few points require clarification. As I discussed in my last book, over the last 30 years, there has been rampant misrepresentation of Bruce Lee's art. A lot of the philosophical notes published in the *Tao* have been taken out of context and twisted to serve a purpose for which they were never meant. Phrases like "using no way as way,"[1] "circle with no circumference,"[2, 3] "the best form is no form",[4] and "learning gained is learning lost"[5, 6] have been used as justification for haphazardly throwing any technique from any other art and mislabeling it as JKD.

What these pseudo JKD instructors aren't telling you is that these philosophical statements have their origins in Zen Buddhism,[7] and placed in that context, they take on an entirely different meaning. One of the basic tenets of Zen Buddhism is that the physical cannot be separated from the spiritual. It's fine to spew philosophy but if you do not have a physical, tangible vehicle through which to test and express it, it is utterly meaningless. Zen is both principle and physical experience. You cannot divorce one from the other. D.T. Suzuki explains this beautifully in *Zen and Japanese Culture*:

> *"But we must know that it is not enough just to see what the Mind is, we must put into practice all that makes it up in our daily life. We may talk about it glibly, we may write books to explain it, but that is far from enough. However much we may talk about water and describe it quite intelligently, that does not make it real water. So with fire. Mere talking of it will not make the mouth burn. To know what they are means to experience them in actual concreteness. A book on cooking will not cure hunger. To feel satisfied we must have actual food. So long as we do not go beyond mere talking, we are not true knowers."*[8]

The problem with our charlatan JKD "masters" is that they never really bothered to learn the physical aspects of JKD. This demonstrates not only a blatant lack of respect for Bruce Lee but a complete misunderstanding of the message he was trying to convey. Levels of transcendence cannot be reached unless you have something to transcend. This is the vehicle by which you practice Zen—be it swordsmanship, tea ceremony, or JKD. But you first must learn the rules before you can transcend them. This is the trouble with saying that JKD is anything you want it to be. If this were the case, then there is no discipline to learn! And with no discipline, there is no way to practice Zen or to understand the philosophical underpinnings of JKD.

There are those who argue that there is no structure to JKD. But once again, this is Bruce Lee taken out of context. Lee himself wrote:

> *"People often mistakenly [believe] that JKD is against form. I don't think I'll go into detail on that, as other paragraphs will clarify that. One thing we must understand: that is, there is always a most efficient and alive manner to carry out a movement (and that the basic laws of leverage, body position, balance, footwork, and so forth, are not to be violated). However, alive, efficient form is one thing; sterile classical sets that bind and condition are another. Aside from the above mentioned, one must also distinguish the subtlety between 'having no form' and having 'no-form.' The first is ignorance, the second transcendence."*[9]

You cannot move from ignorance to transcendence without first learning the "basic laws," and yet, this is exactly what so many would-be JKD masters are preaching. Now it could be argued that counterfeit JKD is its own discipline because techniques are taught. But it is *not* JKD. And it most certainly has nothing to do with Bruce Lee. There's no crime in investigating other arts or techniques. And it is certainly admirable to spend time and energy in the pursuit of excellence in any endeavor.

But I've said this before, and I will continue to say it until my dying day—you cannot throw in techniques from any art you please and call it JKD. Nor can you take an art like wing chun and mislabel it as JKD. To do so is disrespectful to both Bruce Lee and to wing chun masters, or to any other art from which techniques are pilfered and then mislabeled. It also contributes to the destruction of one man's entire life's work. There are indeed basic physical techniques and laws that comprise the art that Bruce Lee spent his lifetime developing.

The technical evidence for what JKD really is, is outlined in *The Straight Lead*, where it is apparent through Bruce Lee's own writings that JKD's origins are in Western boxing and fencing and that Lee was, in fact, looking to develop an art that was a complete departure from wing chun.

You will notice that there are no grappling techniques in this book. There is a reason for this. As Ted Wong knows firsthand, it was not something that Lee emphasized in his own training. With the exception of a few wrestling diagrams and references to joint locks, which have been published, there are hardly any notes on the subject in Lee's personal writings. This is not to say that grappling is not something Lee would have further explored. The sad truth is that he died before we had a full picture of the art.

I feel that close range skills are essential, but I will not be writing about them under the banner of "JKD." It is not for us to assume what would have been. We cannot guess at what direction Lee would have gone and presume to label it as JKD. We must trace everything back to the evidence that was left behind—his writings. Again, there is nothing wrong with exploring other techniques, but do not cite elements that you cannot trace to Bruce Lee and mislabel them as JKD.

The "conceptualization" of JKD really runs counter to everything that Bruce Lee was about. What is so offensive about this blatant misrepresentation is that it flies in the face of Bruce Lee's own writings which tell us to "daily minimize instead of daily decrease,"[10] and to "simply simplify,"[11] In reality, JKD consists of about 5 punches, 3 kicks, and a few ground techniques. The reason for this is incredibly simple. When the pressure's on, you cannot be rifling through a large library of techniques. You need enough techniques to cover all your situations, and then that's it. Everything must be simplified so that in the moment, you do not think. This is the essence of Zen—*mushin* ("no mind").

Unfortunately, many JKD "instructors" have sold Bruce out in the name of profit. To keep their schools running, they teach technique after technique after technique. Even as early as the 1600's, legendary swordsman Miyamoto Musashi knew the folly of this approach when he wrote the following:

> *"Teaching people a large number of sword techniques is turning the way into a business of selling goods, making beginners believe that there is something profound in their training by impressing them with a variety of techniques. This attitude toward strategy must be avoided, because thinking that there is a variety of ways of cutting a man down is evidence of a disturbed mind. In the world, different ways of cutting a man down do not exist. Whether you are an accomplished adept or a noninitiate, a woman or a child, the ways (*michi*) of striking, slapping, and cutting down are not all that numerous. Apart from these movements, there are only those of stabbing and slashing broadly on the horizontal. Because what is primarily at issue is the way (*mishi*) of cutting someone down, there cannot be many differences."[12]*

There may be few ways of cutting a man down, but to perfect those ways, to know how and when to use them, requires an understanding that would allow students to find answers for themselves. Many instructors have not taken the time and effort to develop such an understanding and so are unable to pass this on to their students, and so they keep their students in the dark—and paying the bills—by not giving them the tools that would make them self-sufficient. So the tradition of mediocrity masquerading as mastery continues into the 21st century.

The reason I've gone into this rather lengthy explanation of Zen is that we are about to embark on a journey through the JKD arsenal. You will notice there are only a few techniques, as promised. But we are going to go into each in great detail, explaining the whys, hows, and whens of each. For those who do not understand the Way, this will seem unnecessarily thorough. They will argue that you can go straight from ignorance to transcendence. They are missing a very important step, the most important step—learning. Again, you must learn the rules before you can transcend them.

When Bruce Lee said to discard technique once you've learned it, he didn't mean that you could just forget about it or that you'd never use it again. Nor did he mean that being an artist meant being undisciplined in jumping from technique to technique—or worse, from art to art.

No, in line with Zen philosophy, "discarding" technique would mean that once you've mastered the technical skills, you no longer have to think about them. It is there when you need it. Your body simply reacts. Your mind and body are one, and conscious thought no longer interferes with physical execution. Hence the line from *Enter the Dragon*: "I do not hit. It hits all by itself."

Among Bruce Lee's personal papers, there is a note indicating that Lee intended to write three volumes, each based on a different stage of learning. The note was written in 1970 and read, "Have three volumes, each one corresponding to the three stages, leading to the highest." These "three stages of cultivation" were called "The Stage of Innocence," "The Stage of Art," and "The Stage of Artlessness"[13] The first level, of course, is that of the absolute beginner. Learning is devoid of all self-consciousness and driven by instinct. During the Stage of Art, the student is in the process of technical, physical training. He is learning the nuts and bolts of the art. Because he is consciously programming his body at this stage, his conscious mind will sometimes be at war with his body and hinder performance. As he begins to master the technical aspects of the art, though, he enters the Stage of Artlessness. This is referred to in both Zen literature and Lee's writings as "Prajna Immovable."[14, 15] This is where the natural "no-mindedness" of the master's state is reunited with that of the beginner's. The circle is now complete.

Each of Lee's stages corresponds to the same stages of learning referred to throughout Zen literature. Takuan Soho, as translated by D.T. Suzuki, combined the stages of Innocence and Art into a single category, the stage of Ignorance and Affects. Again, this encompasses the beginning levels through the development of technical knowledge and skill. And the Stage of Artlessness is Prajna Immovable.[16]

The problem with JKD is that everyone talks about Prajna Immovable. Everyone wants to get there. But very few "JKD instructors" are willing to put in the hard work required to understand the Stage of Art before they can get to Artlessness. They're missing the nuts and bolts, the very vehicle that is necessary to understand the philosophy of Zen or JKD.

For all the emphasis on *mushin*, even Takuan Soho reminded us that you cannot achieve it without technical training:

> *"But training in detailed technique is also not to be neglected. The understanding of principle alone cannot lead one to the mastery of movements of the body and its limbs. By practical details I mean as such as what you call the five ways of posing the body, designated each by one character. The principle of spirituality is to be grasped—this goes without saying—but at the same time one must be trained in the technique of swordplay. But training is never to be one-sided. Ri (*li*) and ji (*shih*) are like two wheels of a cart."[17]*

So it is at the stages of Innocence and Art that this book comes in. These are the nuts and bolts of JKD. Again, there aren't a lot of techniques—there aren't supposed to be—but we've gone into quite a bit of detail on the mechanics. Obviously, you are not going to be thinking about mechanics in the heat of battle. But knowing *why* and *how* to perform a technique a certain way will give you a technical advantage. As you progress through the Stage of Art, knowing how something works and putting that knowledge into practice will make you faster, more powerful, and better at reacting with the appropriate response. It places you closer to the stage of Artlessness.

Bruce Lee wrote that "The highest art is no art. The best form is no form."[18] You can see how, if taken out of context, yes, it sounds like he is arguing against the rules of technique. But we know from the passage we quoted earlier that JKD is not against form—that Bruce Lee believed there are, in fact, "basic laws of leverage, body position, balance, footwork" that are "not to be violated."[19] These are the laws presented in this volume.

And now that we've outlined some of the basic principles of Zen philosophy, we can see that the statement "the highest art is no art" comes from the stage of Artlessness. That the "circle with no circumference" isn't just an amorphous nothing existing in a void. No, you must complete the circle, starting from the stage of Innocence and ending at the stage of Artlessness. But first you have to travel through the stage of *Art*. You cannot just proceed from the stage of Innocence straight to the stage of Artlessness.

There are those who will argue that it is futile to invest so much time perfecting so few techniques in such detail. But this, again, runs in direct opposition to what Zen and JKD stand for. To be truly proficient with any skill requires willingness to simplify to a degree that the majority of modern society, with its fascination with novelty, might find pathological. You must refine, refine, refine until you think you think you can do no more—and then refine some more. If you know all of your techniques in such depth, there is no need to look for new ones. With a few tools at your disposal, you must find the answers yourself. You certainly won't find them by jumping from art to art or from teacher to teacher. On this kind of simplicity, Bruce quoted the following from Roger Crosnier:[20]

> *"Simplicity is the height of cultivation and partial cultivation runs to ornamentation. Thus, the closer to the true Way of gung fu, the less wastage of movement. Being good in gung fu does not mean adding more but to be able to get off with sophistication and ornamentation and be simply simple—like a sculptor building a statue, not by adding, but by hacking away the unessential so that the truth will be revealed unobstructed— artlessness."[21]*

In Zen and Japanese Culture, Suzuki quotes Georges Duthuit, who describes how one comes to know Prajna Immovable through the perfection of a single, simple act, the painting of bamboos:

> *"Draw bamboos for ten years, become a bamboo, then forget all about bamboos when you are drawing. In possession of an infallible technique, the individual places himself at the mercy of inspiration."[22]*

And so with this volume, I've given you the tools to develop an infallible technique, as they were developed and practiced by Bruce Lee—and later handed on to me from Sifu Ted Wong. To emphasize the research, methodology, thought, and care that went into Lee's development of his art, I've also outlined the scientific, biomechanical reasons for why these techniques work. I've done so in the hope that you will be able to someday place yourself at the mercy of inspiration.

CHAPTER ONE

BIOMECHANICS 101

This isn't a biomechanics textbook, and it's beyond the scope of this volume to go into the finer details of that science, but an understanding of some basic principles will give you a much better understanding of Jeet Kune Do. On so many fronts, Bruce Lee was light years ahead of his time, and this arena is no exception. Breaking down professional sports to a science may be commonplace these days, but in Lee's time, that kind of analysis was only just beginning. While he may have surveyed many other arts, what he chose to incorporate into his own repertoire was very specific and considered, resulting in an art essentially limited to 4 or 5 punches, 3 or 4 kicks, and a few grappling techniques.

We'll touch on some of the strategic elements later on, but first, we must learn to perform them correctly. And what will help you refine these techniques to perfection is a basic understanding of why Bruce Lee chose to do things a certain way. A lot of people neglect this aspect of the art and move on to application. But failing to build a strong technical foundation is like trying to drive without learning how to put the key in the ignition. It makes no sense, and you'll end up going nowhere. Sloppy technique makes for sloppy application.

It may seem like splitting hairs to break these tools down to a science, but in any sport, knowing how to refine your skills will give you a competitive edge that could make all the difference. For sprinters, a millisecond means victory or defeat. The martial arts should be no different. Honing your skills will result in more speed, more power, and more successful application of those skills. While it's true the number of fast twitch muscle fibers you have is genetically predetermined, you can level the playing field somewhat and do the best with what you've got by refining your technique.

Also if you're in this for the long haul, knowing the basics of biomechanics can save your body a lot of wear and tear. Proper technique and knowledge of what makes those techniques sound can increase your longevity. I always look to Ted Wong as a great example of this. He's honed these skills for over thirty years. As of this writing, he's 70 years old and while almost all of his contemporaries have fallen by the wayside or declined markedly in their performance, he still spars with blokes less than half his age and complains of few aches and pains. He'll tell you that when he first started, before he'd refined his technique, how his body hurt so much he seriously contemplated quitting the martial arts altogether. He also hits a lot harder than he did in the 1960's. If you compare footage of him then and now, you'll see that he can attribute this longevity to analysis and improvement of his skills over the years.

So how do we go about refining technique? The first step is to know why a specific technique is performed the way it is. In this book, we are going to show you why a Bruce Lee punch or kick was so effective. True, the man was born with some serious fast-twitch muscle fibers. But he was also relentless in the refinement of his technique.

Before we can fully describe each technique, though, we need to know some basic principles of biomechanics. We'll briefly explain some of these laws and then we'll see how they apply to all JKD techniques. Later, as we discuss the specifics of each technique, you may want to refer back to this section.

BIOMECHANICS AND FORCE

The term *biomechanics* basically is the science of forces and how they affect humans. A *force* is either a push or a pull that can act *externally* on an object in the environment (i.e. throwing a punch on a heavy bag is a pushing force on the bag) or *internally* within a system or object (i.e. muscles create pulling forces around joints causing movement of your limbs).

TYPES OF MOTION

Motion or movement may be defined as a change in position. There are three kinds of motion. ***Linear motion*** is defined as having all points on a body or object move the same distance in the same direction and at the same time. Simply put for our purposes, this is movement in a straight line. For example, jumping up and down is linear. The trajectory of a straight punch is linear. On the other hand, the trajectory of a hook is circular (Figures 1.1–1.3). This is called ***angular motion*** and occurs when all points on a body or object move about the same axis.[1] Finally, we have ***general motion***, which is a combination of both linear and angular motion. Most human movement falls under this category, and in fact, all of our JKD techniques combine elements of both. All JKD kicks and punches include linear vertical, linear horizontal, and angular components.

Figure 1.1 **Figure 1.2** **Figure 1.3**

Types of motion—*The straight lead (Figure 1.1) and vertical uppercut (Figure 1.2) are mostly linear in motion, while the hook is largely angular, or rotational in motion. As we'll see in future chapters, however, there are elements of both motion types in all punches.*

FORCE PRODUCTION

In layman's terms, velocity and speed are interchangeable. It is important to note, however, that speed is merely distance traveled over time. Velocity is a measure of both speed and direction and is represented in physics studies as a vector quantity. Vector quantities are drawn as arrows and show you two things—how fast and in what direction. The length of the arrow represents speed—for example, 1 centimeter might represent 20 km/hr. And direction of the arrow represents direction of the object. If an object is moving in two directions, you can draw a triangle and find the sum of the two vectors by solving for what we call the ***resultant*** using the parallelogram rule.

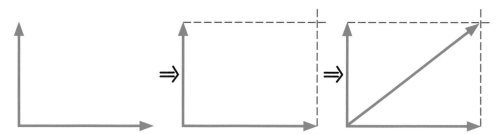

Hewitt, *Conceptual Physics*, Ninth Edition.
Copyright © 2002 Pearson Education, Inc., publishing as Addison Wesley. All rights reserved

Figure 1.4

Solving for the resultant

$$R = \sqrt{(V^2 + H^2)}$$

Velocity is important because a change in direction and/or speed is called *acceleration* and in force production, acceleration is the name of the game. In most sports, success depends on generating the most acceleration before applying force to another object. In tennis, the object of service technique is to generate maximum acceleration of the racquet head at impact. In the baseball or golf swing, again, the object is to maximize acceleration of the bat or club when you strike the ball. The same goes for throwing punches. The object is not only to move your fist or foot at a high velocity, but to have that velocity maximally increase at the point of impact. This is known as Newton's Second Law of Motion which states that the acceleration produced by a net force on a body is directly proportional to the magnitude of the net force, is in the same direction as the net force, and is inversely proportional to the mass of the body.[2] In mathematical terms, it is expressed as:

$$\text{Force} = \text{mass} \times \text{acceleration}$$

From the equation, we see that force production increases with acceleration. We also see that an increase in mass of the object that is accelerating also increases force. This is central to all the techniques that comprise JKD, which I affectionately call "the art of how to best throw your weight around." For every punch and every kick, you should be asking yourself how you can get as much of your body weight into the technique without compromising balance and mobility.

In the following chapters, we'll explain what Bruce Lee believed to be the best ways to maximize acceleration and body weight into each technique. We'll explain how a 135-pound Bruce Lee could generate such incredible power. Bruce himself wrote in the *Tao*:

> *"The principle is to preserve the maximum acceleration up to the last instant of contact.*
> *Regardless of distance, the final phase of a movement should be the fastest."*[3]

IMPULSE AND SNAPPINESS

Related to the equation for Newton's Second Law is an equation that accounts for a change in velocity—and in the case of throwing punches, a change in direction. Momentum is defined as the following equation:

$$\text{Momentum} = \text{mass} \times \text{velocity}$$

To change an object's momentum, the velocity must change as well. When you throw a punch, the punch does not continue forever in the same direction unless you're Mr. Fantastic. No, you have to retract your hand at some point. This requires a change in direction. For straight punches, this means throwing the punch straight out, hitting the target, and then bringing the hand back to the on-guard position. We've already established that force is a product of mass and acceleration. But there's another variable here—how long do we apply force to an object to maximize force production?

Let's use the equation for Newton's Second Law and for acceleration, we'll use the average acceleration. This is the initial velocity (v_i) (which in the case of our punch is when the hand starts moving towards the target) minus the final velocity (v_f) (the velocity at impact) divided by the time duration of force application:

$$\text{Average acceleration} = \frac{\text{final velocity} - \text{initial velocity}}{\text{time interval}}$$

Remember Newton's Second Law is expressed as:

$$\text{Force} = \text{mass} \times \text{acceleration}$$

PROJECTILE MOTION

In discussions of martial arts technique, you hear a lot about torque, force, mass, acceleration, and stability. But you never hear about projectile motion. Yet this is a concept central to most JKD techniques, and it has to do with footwork. A *projectile* is any object that has been thrown or dropped into the air and once in the air, the only force acting on it, barring significant air resistance, is gravity. A lot of the time in JKD, the projectile is you! Every time you push step or push off, you are momentarily—even if it's only for a millisecond—in the air. Your toes might still be barely touching the ground, but the majority of your body weight is airborne. Every time you throw a straight punch, and almost any time you throw any punch, your body itself becomes a projectile giving you more force production by allowing you to throw your body weight into it.

So let's look a little closer at projectile motion. Once you've thrown an object—in this case, your body—into the air, that's it, you cannot change directions in midair. The only force acting on you at this point is gravity, which we know to have an acceleration of 9.81 m/s/s downward or –9.81 m/s/s.

I won't bore you with the derivation of the equations for projectile motion, but there is an excellent explanation of it in McGinnis' *Biomechanics of Sport and Exercise* for those of you who are interested.[5]

For our purposes, just knowing what the equation is for vertical velocity of a projectile should be enough:

$$v_f = v_i + g\Delta t$$

Where:

v_f = final vertical velocity
v_i = initial vertical velocity
Δt = change in time
g = -9.81 m/s/s

Now, if you look at this equation carefully, it should look familiar. Remember from algebra class:

$$y = mx + b$$

It's that trusty parabolic equation where –9.8 m/s/s is the slope of the line. Again, we won't go into all the mathematical details here. Just know that whenever you push off or launch yourself into the air, even if it's just for a fraction of a second, your body is following a parabolic pathway. And at any point on that path, you have both a vertical and horizontal velocity. The horizontal displacements for each time interval, by the way, are equal, creating that symmetrical parabolic path.

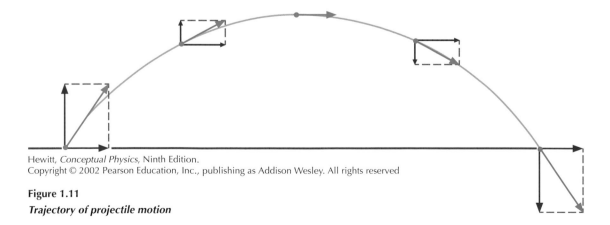

Figure 1.11
Trajectory of projectile motion

What does all of this have to do with JKD? Well, first we mentioned footwork. There are three things that determine what kind of parabola we have: time spent airborne, peak height, and horizontal distance covered (also known as horizontal displacement). In his discussions of footwork, Bruce stresses the importance of small steps. The reason? You'll be able to shift direction much faster. Yes, there's even an equation for this:

$$\text{Horizontal displacement} = \text{initial horizontal velocity} \times \text{flight time}$$

So you can see the bigger your step, the longer time you spend in the air. And remember once you've launched yourself into the air, you are at the mercy of gravity. You cannot change your direction until you come back down. So the less push off you give yourself, the less time you'll spend in the air, and the less distance you'll cover—small steps. There will be times, of course, when the situation will call for you to cover greater distance with your footwork, but in general, keep those steps small and controlled.

Projectile motion is not only used to explain shiftiness, though. It's a law that is central to punching power. As you'll see in our discussion of the punches, when you push off with the back leg, you always want to hit the target before your front foot hits the ground. The reason is easily explained by projectile motion. Remember, force is a product of mass and acceleration. Acceleration is a change in velocity. At any point on the projectile parabola, you have both a vertical and horizontal velocity, and you are accelerating towards the ground. If you wait until you stop and hit the ground, you will no longer be accelerating towards the target. You no longer have a velocity in the direction of the target and you've missed out on using all the body weight that gravity was pulling on. How are you going to produce force for that punch now?

If you do hit the target before you and your front foot land, you take advantage of throwing all your body weight into the punch. You have both horizontal velocity and gravity on your side. You're accelerating, baby.

With footwork, with or without an accompanying punch, it's best to minimize your time in flight so that you will stay close to the ground and mobile. So how high should you push off? It's been found in studies with shot-putters that the resultant velocity increases—and, thus, acceleration and force increase—when the shot is released at an angle of less than 45°.[6] To maximize horizontal velocity and minimize "hang time," then, the same goes for you when you "release" yourself as a projectile from the ground. This has to do with air resistance. The higher you launch yourself, the more you are actually held up, to some degree, by air resistance. This is exactly what we don't want. What we're aiming for is to cover as much ground as possible with the least amount of time in the air. You'll have to experiment with this on your own to find what is most efficient for you.

Figure 1.12   Figure 1.13   Figure 1.14

Figure 1.15   Figure 1.16   Figure 1.17

***Projectile motion**—As I come out of a kick (Figures 1.12–1.13) and launch into a straight lead, the trajectory of my body follows that of projectile motion (Figures 1.14–1.17). I am moving both upwards (by a few inches) and forward. In Figure 1.16 I am airborne at the point of contact, allowing me to project force, both downward and straight-ahead, into the punch.*

WORK AND POWER

From our discussion of impulse, you know that the impulse is the product of force and time. We can also measure another variable—the distance an object moves when a force is applied to it. The product of this distance and the force is known as ***work*** and the equation is:

$$\text{Work} = \text{force} \times \text{distance}$$

Whenever you step and slide and cover a certain amount of ground, work is being done. Whenever you throw a kick, your muscles contract, producing forces that pull on your tendons and bones. This causes your leg to move through space. Your leg covers a specific distance. That's work.

Crucial to the biomechanics of the martial arts is the rate at which you can do work. We call this ***power***. In layman's terms, we often interchange this with the word force and we will do so in this book, but in "biomechanicspeak," they are two very different things. The equation for power is as follows:

$$\text{Power} = \frac{\text{work}}{\text{time}}$$

Power, as you can imagine, is very important to us. It doesn't really help us to throw a kick if it's so slow it never reaches the target. Just think of Bruce Lee and how fast he moved his limbs through space. He was power personified.

KINETIC ENERGY

In the realm of biomechanics, *energy* is defined as the capacity to do work. As you may recall from high school physics, mechanical energy comes in two forms: 1) *kinetic energy*, which is energy of motion and 2) *potential energy*, which is energy due to position.

When an object moves, its motion gives it an ability to do work. The movement gives it kinetic energy. If you hit a heavy bag, your moving fist has kinetic energy, the ability to displace the bag. Kinetic energy is determined by an object's mass and velocity. The mathematical equation is:

$$\text{Kinetic energy} = \tfrac{1}{2}(\text{mass} \times \text{velocity}^2)$$

This equation makes measuring kinetic energy much easier than measuring force, as we often know the mass and velocity of objects. Measuring acceleration is not always so easy.[7]

In the case of hitting the heavy bag, the equation makes sense. The faster you hit the bag, the more capacity you have for moving it. And the more body weight—or mass—you put behind your punch, the more you'll displace it.

POTENTIAL ENERGY: THE ENERGY OF GOOD FORM

In scientific terms, potential energy is often defined as energy of position. How appropriate! Throughout Bruce Lee's writings, you'll see reference after reference to good form, alignment, position. In the following chapters, we'll be spending a lot of time describing the proper stance, and the mechanics of each technique. Some of this is strategic, of course, but the underlying principle is that we are trying to create the most potential energy without sacrificing efficiency or safety (i.e. mobility, stability, etc.)

There are two types of potential energy that we'll be discussing repeatedly. The first is *gravitational potential energy*. Elevating objects against gravity requires work. So once an object is elevated, it has additional potential energy. Just as we explained in the case of projectile motion, we want to use gravity to our advantage as often as we can. The equation for this is:

$$\text{Gravitational potential energy} = \text{mass} \times \text{gravitational acceleration} \times \text{height}$$

So, in our example of the straight lead and projectile motion, when you push off, you temporarily elevate yourself above the ground. In that airborne position, you have more gravitational potential energy to direct in your punch. This is essentially what Jack Dempsey described as the "falling step." By "falling," you allow gravity to take you downward and into the punch. In his book, Championship Fighting, Dempsey uses the analogy of a sled to explain gravitational potential energy:

> "In a sense, the boy and his sled are falling objects. But the slope of the hill prevents them from falling straight down. Their fall is deflected to the angle of the hill. The direction of their weight-in-motion is on a slant. And when they reach the level plain at the bottom of the hill, they will continue to slide for a while. However, the direction of their slide on the plain—the direction of their weight-in-motion—will be straight out, at a right angle to the straight-down pull of gravity."[8]

We'll come back to this idea of gravitational potential energy again and again in our chapter on footwork. By positioning your upper body in a certain way, you create more gravitational potential energy for yourself with accompanying footwork. In many cases you offset your weight just enough to help you move in a particular direction with more speed and less effort, all compliments of earth's gravitational pull.

Figure 1.18

Gravitational potential energy*—By leaning
slightly backward and lifting my back foot, I am
increasing my potential gravitational energy. I
can now essentially fall into the step. Gravity
does all the work, and I move faster while
expending less energy.*

Bruce Lee spent a lot of time in developing the JKD stance. Of course, he was incorporating strategic factors (e.g. narrow and closed stance, stability, etc.), but the stance also was designed to maximize potential energy, specifically for throwing the straight lead. As we'll soon discuss, the correct on-guard position, is positioning of your body to throw the most effective punch—for example, hip position for uncoiling of the body during rotation, foot position to maximize the push off and, thus, gravitational potential energy, and a slight lean forward to cheat inertia. All are examples of maximizing potential energy.

STRAIN ENERGY: THE SLINGSHOT EFFECT

The other type of potential energy important to understanding JKD is called ***strain energy***. This is potential energy generated by the deformation of an object. Think of a slingshot or a rubber band. The further you stretch you it, the further you deform it, and the more capacity it has to do work. In discussions of the martial arts, we sometimes interchange the term strain energy with leverage. Strain energy is dependent on the degree of the object's deformation and the stiffness of the object, which may also be referred to as the spring constant of the material.

Strain energy is mathematically represented by the equation:

$$SE = \tfrac{1}{2}(k\Delta x^2)$$

Where:

SE = strain energy
K = stiffness or spring constant of material
Δx = change in length or deformation of the object from its normal position[9]

From the equation, we see that the greater the deformation, the greater the potential energy. In the *Tao*, Bruce Lee describes strain energy as it relates to throwing a ball:

"The arm is kept so far behind that the chest muscles pulling against it are tensed and stretched. The final wrist snap is postponed until the last instant before release or in striking, before contact. In football, the punter puts the last snap into his knee and foot as, or a shade after, he makes contact with the ball." [10]

Figure 1.19 **Figure 1.20** **Figure 1.21**

Strain energy in hooking techniques—*In hook punching, the hip always precedes the hand. This creates tension at the shoulder, producing potential strain energy (Figure 1.19). The same principle applies to the hook kick. Tension is placed on the hip joint by taking the leg up so that the knee never overtakes the hip or the centerline (Figure 1.20). At the point of impact, you still maintain this tension (Figure 1.21). It isn't until after you've kicked through the target that the knee overtakes the hip.*

In JKD, for example, strain energy is especially important for throwing hook punches. As we'll discuss in a future chapter, you never want to let your arm overtake your hip as you rotate into the punch. In a later chapter, we'll be referring to a "catch" you should feel on your shoulder as your hip momentarily rotates away from your arm. This creates tension, or strain, on the tendons of your chest and shoulder. You are stretching, or deforming, those tendons, so you can store more potential energy for the punch. The same goes for hook kicks. Your knee should never move ahead of your hip. Keeping the knee a hair behind the front hip increases the strain on the tendons of your leg at the hip. By keeping your leg stretched and rigid until the last minute, you'll be able to generate "snap" in your kicks.

Figure 1.22 **Figure 1.23**

Last instant before contact—*In Figure 1.22 my hip is at full extension. At the last moment before impact I let the lower leg whip out at the knee joint.*

This is also why flexibility is so important. The more you can stretch, or deform, the muscles and tendons, the more strain energy you can store. Of course, if the strain is too great, this can lead to pulled muscles, torn ligaments, and ruptured tendons. Again, flexibility will help minimize such injuries while increasing the potential energy and force of your kicks and punches.

ENERGY, WORK, AND MOMENTUM: GIVE A LITTLE TO GET A LITTLE

From our earlier explanation of impulse, remember that impulse is a change in momentum. In JKD, whenever we throw a punch or kick, we are looking to maximize the velocity and acceleration of our fist or foot. Recall the equation for impulse:

$$Ft = \text{impulse}$$

Also remember that this was derived from the following:

$$\text{Force} \times \text{time interval} = \text{mass} \times (\text{final velocity} - \text{initial velocity})$$

It follows, then, that the greater the change in velocity, the greater the force production. How does this relate to work? Remember that work is the product of force and displacement. Greater displacement, or increased work, allows for a greater change in velocity. This is why the rear cross is often thought of as boxing's big gun. Your body has more room to rotate, and your fist has a greater distance to travel to the target. Your hand goes through a much larger displacement throwing a cross than it does throwing a jab. That larger displacement, or greater distance covered, means that more work is being done. It also means more force production.

In fighting applications, of course, there is always a compromise between power and speed. You don't want your hand to go through such a displacement that the moving target moves out of the way! You also don't want to wind up so your punches become telegraphic. But, depending on your body position, you can take advantage of doing more work to get more force. For example, coming out of a hook, you are naturally set up to throw a cross with greater room for hip rotation than usual. Or vice versa, after you've thrown a cross, you're set up to throw a hook (Figures 1.24–1.26). You've already rotated considerably clockwise, so you've got a lot of room from which to uncoil counterclockwise into the hook. Your hand travels a greater distance so you can pack more into your punch.[11]

Figure 1.24 **Figure 1.25** **Figure 1.26**

Displacement and velocity—After throwing a cross (Figure 1.24), I am in an open stance, placing me farther from the target. Because my fist has more distance to travel (larger displacement), this allows for a greater change in velocity (acceleration). This makes it possible to generate much more force throwing a hook following a cross than throwing a hook from a regular closed stance.

NEWTON'S FIRST LAW OF MOTION: INERTIA

Before we progress any further, we must address the issue of inertia. As Newton's First Law of Motion states, an object continues in a state of rest, or of uniform motion in a straight line, unless it is compelled to change that state by forces impressed upon it.[12] In the martial arts, then, this is especially important because the speed with which you initiate an action, either defensive or offensive, is crucial.

Obviously, this is where good form is so important. The less extraneous movement in your techniques, the faster you will be. This is why we always stress refinement of your skills. We are only born with so many fast twitch muscle fibers. But you can improve your speed by refining your technique. Even the smallest increments of refinement can pay off with exponentially increased speed.

Another way to overcome inertia is to manipulate the placement of your center of gravity. In our chapter on the straight lead, for instance, we'll discuss how a slight lean forward helps you, in effect, cheat inertia. By slightly offsetting your center of gravity towards the direction in which you want to move, you put gravity to work for you. You are essentially falling into a punch. This means more force production and less effort, a pretty good deal. The idea is very similar to a runner at the starting block. When a sprinter moves from the "on your mark" position to the "get set" position, he shifts his center of gravity up and to the furthest point forward within his base of support. This allows him to overcome inertia most efficiently. This is ideal for explosive movement in one direction, but not so great if you have to be ready to move in any direction. In the case of the straight lead, just prior to throwing it, you know you'll be moving linearly. Though not nearly to the degree that the runner does, you shift your line of gravity slightly forward. In his notes, Bruce wrote that this shifting of your center of gravity is to be used when you know you're in attack mode:

Figure 1.27

Cheating inertia—*By leaning slightly to the left as I pick up my left foot, I get a head start on inertia. The position of my upper body and a little help from gravity help me overcome inertia and get me moving faster.*

"For an attack, the center of gravity should imperceptibly be shifted to the front foot in order to allow the back leg and foot freedom for the shortest, fastest and most explosive lunge."[13]

You'll see this idea of cheating inertia again and again. In the footwork chapter, we'll discuss certain moves that are aided by a slight shift in weight. For example, when reversing direction with a side step, if you lean slightly with the upper body in the reverse direction and then sidestep with both feet momentarily off the ground, you fall towards the desired direction (Figure 1.27). If you were moving in one direction, left for instance, remember this is a form of linear inertia. To move right, then, you've got to impose a force. You won't have to work so hard to impose that force if you let gravity do a lot of the work for you.

The same principle applies to defensive moves like bobbing and weaving. When you weave, a slight lean at the waist sets the majority of your body weight into motion. Again, gravity will be pulling on you and helping you along. In the section on kicking, you'll see that a slight lean forward and the placement of your body weight in the front foot will help you generate the torque needed to get your leg up quickly to kick.

The law of inertia applies to both linear and rotational motion. In both cases, mass is directly proportional to the degree of an object's inertia. The more massive an object, the more force is required to move it. Think of heavyweights versus featherweights and notice how much faster the smaller fighters are. It takes a lot more energy and force to move around 200 pounds as opposed to 126 pounds. This explains how smaller fighters are still able to generate tremendous power. They are capable of accelerating their body weight better than larger fighters. Remember that force increases with acceleration. For every fighter there is an optimal balance between weight, force, and speed. Greater weight, or mass, may mean more force, but at some point, too much will compromise speed, and consequently, force. Too little weight may mean not enough force behind punches or enough muscle to move body parts fast enough to accelerate adequately.

In rotational, or angular motion, there is another factor besides mass that impacts inertia. With angular motion, an object rotates about an axis. In JKD, our angular punches include hooks and uppercuts. The most important thing to remember about ***rotary inertia*** is that the greater the distance between the rotating object and its axis of rotation, the greater the rotational inertia. This is also referred to as the ***radial distribution of mass***[14] (Figures 1.28–1.29).

To illustrate this, think of a figure skater going into a spin. To increase his spin rate, he draws in his arms and legs, decreasing rotary inertia, or resistance. This increases angular velocity. To slow down and come out of the spin, he spreads his arms and legs out, increasing rotary inertia. His body mass is distributed farther away from the axis of rotation. There are notes in the *Tao* that address this principle in relation to other sports:

> *"After momentum in a throwing or elliptical striking movement has been generated by a long radius and a long arc in the swing, the speed may be increased without applying additional force by suddenly shortening the radius of the arc. This effect is seen in the 'pull-in' at the last of the arc in the hammer throw, in the backward thrust against the forward leg by the batter in baseball, and so on. Snapping a towel or a whip are common examples of the same 'shortened lever' principle."[15]*

The same rule applies to fighters throwing hook punches. The tighter your hook, the closer your arm is to your body, the faster you can turn into the punch. And since hooks are usually for close quarters work, you want to make yourself small anyway. Keeping your hooks tight makes you more elusive, faster, and more powerful. This is all related to the radial distribution of mass. And once again, developing your punches so as to minimize motion and maximize efficiency is a matter of refining proper technique.

Figure 1.28

Figure 1.29

Radial distribution—*The hook punch has a much shorter radius because our arms are shorter than our legs (Figure 1.28). A bent-arm hook further shortens this radius between the rotating object (the hand) and the axis of rotation (my centerline and torso). The shorter the radius, the tighter the punch and greater the acceleration. Radial distribution is one reason why hook kicks tend to be slower than hook punches. There is a greater distance from the axis of rotation to the rotating object, which is the foot (Figure 1.29). There is also more inertia to overcome because there is more mass to move.*

TORQUE

Since we've just been discussing rotary inertia, now would be a good time to introduce the subject of torque. *Torque* is a force that is specifically rotational and results in a turning effect. Mathematically, it is represented by the equation:

Torque = lever arm x force

Just as the velocity of a rotating object is dependent on a distance variable, torque depends on the distance from the line of force to the axis of rotation. This distance is called the *lever arm*. It is also referred to as the *moment arm* or the *perpendicular distance*. A good example of this would be a door swinging on its hinges. If you exert a force on the door by pushing it on the side of the door close to the hinges—the axis of rotation—notice how hard you have to push to open the door. If, on the other hand, you push the door at the point furthest from the hinges—where door knobs and door handles are always placed—notice how relatively easy it is to open the door. In accordance with our equation, you can produce the same amount of torque with a large force and a small perpendicular distance, or a small amount of force and a greater perpendicular distance.

The angular force, or torque, produced by a hook punch is very similar. In any sport, torque, particularly hip rotation, is an elemental component of technique. Think of the golf swing, the tennis forehand, baseball's tabletop swing, and the football pass. All involve some kind of hip rotation, which is initiated by force produced by the body.

Figure 1.30

Figure 1.31

Figure 1.32

Figure 1.33

Figure 1.34

Force couple—*A great example of a force couple is the basic straight-lead-straight-kick combo. After throwing the lead hand (Figure 1.30) all my weight is shifted forward. I move into the kick quickly by applying force to opposite, noncolinear directions. To do this, I simultaneously pull in the hand and push off with the back foot (Figure 1.31). If both hands were moving in opposite directions, they would still be linear to each other. And if the right hand and left foot were moving in the same direction, we would have noncolinear forces but not in opposition to each other. No, for a force couple, we must have the lead hand pulling in and the left pushing in the opposite direction. These are both opposing and noncolinear. This allows me to quickly shift my center of gravity from the front of my base of support (Figure 1.30) to the back (Figure 1.32–1.34).*

In our discussion of rotary inertia, recall that there is a trade-off between mass, velocity, and force production. Similarly, with torque there is a trade-off between the lever arm, force, and angular force. When throwing a hook, then, the tighter the hook, the more force must be applied to generate a certain amount of torque. When throwing a loose hook, where the arm is more extended, you can potentially throw a punch with just as much angular force and less effort. For strategic purposes, though, even though it requires a tremendous amount of energy, it is usually more advantageous to throw tight hooks for reasons we've already outlined—speed, explosiveness, and evasion. However, there will be times, when a loose hook, with its increased lever arm, increased torque, and whip-like action, will be an effective choice.[16] Torque is not just important to the angular punches like hooks and uppercuts. Hip rotation is crucial to all punches— including straight ones—and all kicks, as we'll see in upcoming chapters. The increased perpendicular distance in kicking is one of the reasons why kicks can generate so much more power than punches. The distance from your hips and the axis of rotation to your foot is much greater than the distance between the axis and your hand. However, most people move their upper body limbs much faster than their lower limbs because the legs carry so much more mass. It's the old mass-versus-speed balancing act.

In addition to the torque generated by hip rotation, there is also a kind of torque that is very important to kicking. It is generated by what we call a *force couple*, which consists of two forces acting in opposite directions. To illustrate a force couple, think of a book lying flat on a tabletop. If you were to push the book to the right at the lower left corner and simultaneously push it to the left at the top right corner, the book would spin counterclockwise. The two forces are moving in opposite directions and are noncolinear. (If they were colinear, you would be pushing at both lower corners in opposite directions and the book wouldn't move).

What do force couples have to do with kicking? Well, to get your front leg off the ground quickly you'll actually need to generate a bit of torque. We'll get into more detail in the kicking chapter, but what you're essentially doing is pushing slightly upward with the back foot and pulling by first digging into the ground with the front foot. At the same time, you are redirecting your center of gravity from a forward more upright position to your back leg and downward. You are doing the same thing the book does on the tabletop. Your limbs are rotating about your center of gravity as you shift from having the weight in the front foot to placing it in the back. The push-pull action helps you generate the torque that makes it possible to get your leg up into kicking position (Figures 1.30–1.34)

BALANCE AND STABILITY

As we've seen throughout Bruce Lee's writings, balance is a key component of JKD and one of what Bruce termed its "underlying ingredients."[17] An object is said to be *balanced* or in stable equilibrium if its line of gravity falls within its base of support.[18] *Stability* refers to the degree to which an athlete can resist having his balance disturbed. In any fighting situation, balance and stability are important for so many reasons. If you are unbalanced in any way, it is difficult to be in a position to either attack or evade. Without stability, it is impossible to generate adequate force in punches and kicks, and it's a lot easier to be knocked down. Before we further explore these definitions, let's define a few other terms first.

We keep referring to center of gravity throughout this chapter, so let's define it. The *center of gravity* of an object is that point on an object around which its weight is evenly distributed. We can think of this as that area of the body where most of our mass is concentrated. For our purposes, this is almost always at some location at the core, or trunk, of the body—basically, anywhere on the body that is not a limb. Our limbs, however, carry quite a bit of weight, and when they shift, so does our center of gravity. For example, if you raise your hands above your head, your center of gravity, while still located at some location at your core, shifts up. When you move your right arm out to your side, your center of gravity shifts to the right. When you weave to the left, your center of gravity moves slightly to the left. When you duck into a crouch and bend your knees, you lower your center of gravity (Figure 1.35).

Figure 1.35
Lowering center of gravity

The next term we need to define is the ***base of support.*** In sports biomechanics, this is the area on the ground defined by the athlete's point of contact. In our case, this would be the area determined by our foot position.[19] If you were to draw a line from an object's center of gravity straight down to the ground, that line should fall within the base of support. We say the object is balanced. This is what we call the ***line of gravity.*** If, however, the line falls outside the base of support, we say the object is unbalanced.

This is a fundamental element of all JKD techniques. One of the most common mistakes among students just learning to throw the straight lead is that they allow their center of gravity to overtake their base of support. They think that because it is a linear punch, they must throw their weight forward. This is partially true, but as we'll see in a subsequent chapter, this has more to do with hurtling your entire body weight forward via projectile motion. To maintain balance, though, you can never let your trunk overtake your feet. A good way to test this is to stop yourself after throwing a punch—it works for the cross, too—and look down at the floor. If you see that you're overlooking your knee, you're okay. But if you find yourself looking at a point on the floor that is in front of your knee, you're in trouble.

The same is also true for defensive moves like the bob and weave. A lot of beginners start out by weaving too far to either side. Their trunks sway outside the base of support making the move awkward and unbalanced. You can use the same test for this. Weave to the left and stop. Look down. Are you looking straight down at your knee? If so, you're okay. If you're looking at a point to the left of your left knee, then you're unbalanced. Take it down a notch and minimize your movement.

All JKD techniques require some transfer of weight from one point within the base of support to another. In throwing a hook punch, for example, we often start with more of our weight in the front foot, at the front of our support base, and then shift that weight to the back foot, at the back of the support base, creating a pulling action. You can generate a lot of force while keeping the line of gravity within the base of support.

The real challenge of balance in JKD, though, is maintaining balance and stability over a constantly shifting base of support. From *Commentaries on the Martial Way*:

"Moving properly means carrying out the necessary movement without loss of balance. Until balance is regained, the boxer is ineffective in both attack and defense. Therefore in all movement, balance must be retained." [20]

Figure 1.36   **Figure 1.37**

Balance—*In Figure 1.36 my center of gravity is shifted to the right but still within the base of support determined by my foot position. My head and torso are directly over my right knee and foot. In Figure 1.37, however, my head and torso are shifted too far right. If you were to draw a line from my head to the floor, it would land to the right of my foot, outside the base of support. It would take very little force to knock me over.*

Related to the idea of balance is the property of *stability*. As we mentioned earlier, this is the degree of resistance required to disturb one's balance. There are three variables that affect stability: the height of the object's center of gravity, the size of the base of support, and the object's weight. And, yes, there is an equation to represent this:

Toppling force x moment arm of toppling force = object's weight x moment arm of object

Technically, it's not the width of the base of support that determines stability. More accurately, it's the horizontal distance between the line of gravity and the edge of the base of support in the direction of the toppling force that determines stability. [21] This is the moment arm of the object. The "toppling force" is the force required to unbalance the object. The moment arm of the toppling force is dependent on the object's center of gravity. The higher the object's center of gravity, the longer the moment arm is for toppling the object. Remember, a longer moment arm requires less force to produce torque. Therefore, the lower the object's center of gravity, the shorter the moment arm of the toppling force, and a greater force is required to unbalance the object.

This is a pretty technical explanation of stability. What's important to know is that lowering your center of gravity and widening the base of support usually result in greater stability.

So we've already established that widening the base of support, or in our case, widening the JKD stance, increases stability. But remember Bruce's quote about "movement without loss of balance." Movement. In JKD, your base of support is constantly shifting. As we'll see in the next chapter, the JKD stance is designed to strike a balance between stability and mobility. The wider your stance the more stable and less mobile you'll be. A narrower stance means less stability but more mobility. There is always a trade-off between the two.

 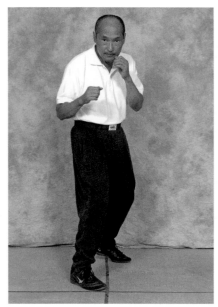

Figure 1.38   **Figure 1.39**

Raising the center of gravity—*A slight raising of the left heel raises your center of gravity making you less stable. Sometimes this is desirable as in the case of overcoming inertia to launch an offensive. Here, Ted's shifted his weight forward and upward much in the same way a runner does at the starting block.*

In certain situations, you'll want to lower your center of gravity and widen your base of support. In close quarters, for example, when you duck, you widen your stance and lower yourself to the ground. Not only does this get you out of harm's way, but you've also hunkered down so that follow up blows are less likely to knock you over. Similarly, if a grappler shoots in to throw you, you'll go into a wrestler's crouch. Again, this widens your stance and lowers your center of gravity. In this position it will take a lot more force to topple you.

Widening the base of support, though, is not just for defensive maneuvers. As we'll see in the next section, whenever you apply a force, an equal and opposite force comes back at you. The more stable your stance, the less likely you'll be thrown off balance by the opposing reaction force.[22] Examples of widening the base of support to apply force can be found in almost all sports. When a pitcher throws a ball, he takes that giant step after the wind up just before releasing the ball. If he didn't, he wouldn't be able to apply as much force to the ball without being thrown off balance. Try hitting a heavy bag while standing on one foot. That's a pretty narrow base of support. You're likely to be knocked off balance. Now stand in a regular stance and hit the bag. You've widened the base of support and can absorb the opposing force of the bag while maintaining stability.

NEWTON'S THIRD LAW OF MOTION: MINIMIZING WEAR AND TEAR
In our analysis of stability, we've just introduced the concept of action and reaction. This is more formally known as Newton's Third Law of Motion, which states:

> *"To every action there is always opposed an equal reaction: or the mutual actions of two bodies upon each other are always equal and directed to contrary parts."*[23]

Going back to our heavy bag example, remember how a stable stance keeps us balanced after we've hit it. When we apply force to the bag, it sends an equal and opposite force right back at us. If our stance lacks stability, we'll be knocked off balance. Think of the recoil of a rifle. The force the rifle exerts on the bullet causes an equal force that acts on the rifle, causing it to kick. The rifle, however, does not move with the same acceleration over the same distance as the bullet, though, because it is so much more massive than the bullet.

In our heavy bag example, then, notice the jarring effect you feel when you hit it. That's the same amount of force that you applied to the bag coming at you. In JKD, we're often in the business of hitting things. Over days, weeks, years, decades, that's a lot of hitting! And if you're connecting, that's a lot of force coming back at you—every time you make contact with a target.

Because of all that pounding, you'll want to construct a stance and develop techniques that help you absorb that reactionary force with the least wear and tear on your body. If you plan to stay in the martial arts for any real length of time, it's in your best interest to adopt practices that minimize the physical stress you'll incur.

This leads us right into the next chapter, where balance, stability, mobility, force production, potential energy, and martial arts longevity all begin—the JKD stance.

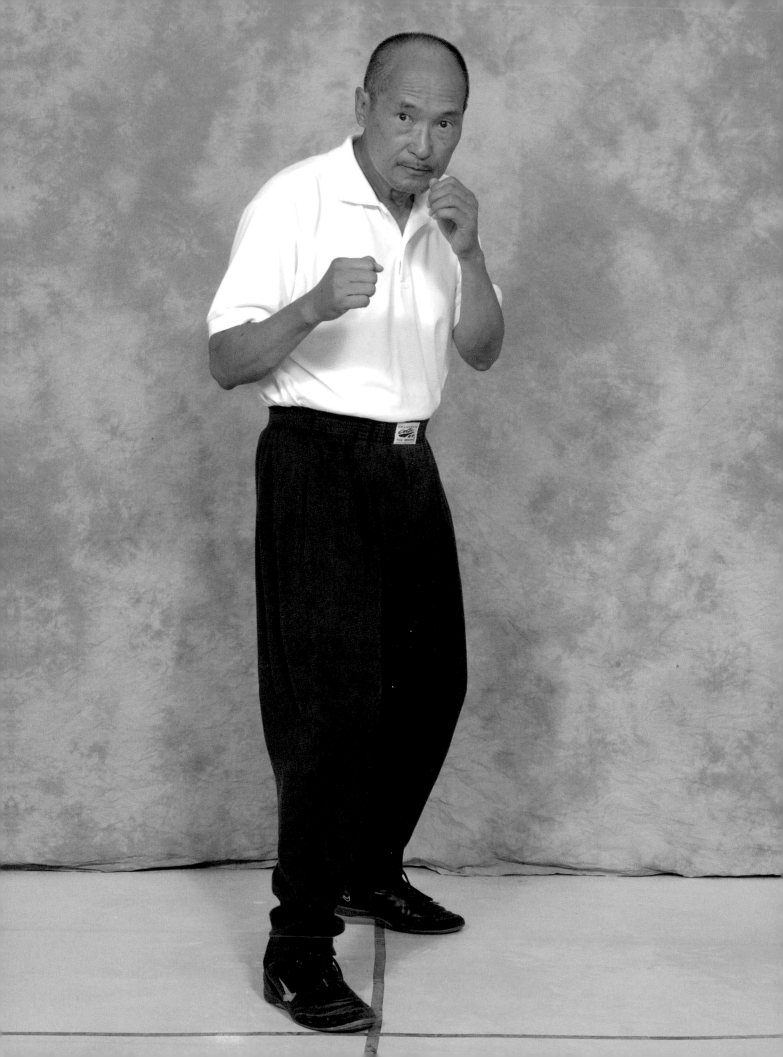

CHAPTER TWO

THE STANCE

The importance of the JKD stance cannot be overemphasized. It is the culmination of a great deal of research and experimentation, and you can actually see its evolution throughout Bruce Lee's films. Notice how wide the stance is in *The Big Boss* and *Fists of Fury* and how it narrows by the time *Game of Death* and *Enter the Dragon* were filmed. Also notice how much more fluid and mobile Bruce is in these later films. It's this stance, in its most advanced form that we'll be exploring here.

In *The Straight Lead*, I traced some of the origins of the JKD stance from Aldo Nadi's raised left heel to Jack Dempsey's and Jim Driscoll's vertical fist. We don't have the space to go into such detail here, so you may want to refer to this earlier book for a better understanding of how Bruce came to design the stance. There are also a few tests and details that we are not able to cover here.[1] The straight lead and the stance that was built around it are so important to JKD, that, yes, we had to give them their own volume.

The main thing to remember about the stance is that you want to be in it as much as possible. It's the safest place to hang out. According to Bruce himself, "No matter in what direction or at what speed you move, your aim is to *retain the fundamental stance* which has been found the most effective for fighting." The very criteria by which we judge a technique and its execution, then, is by how little it deviates from the stance.[2]

HOW TO CONSTRUCT THE STANCE
The following sections detail the finer points of constructing a rock solid JKD Stance.

Strong Side Forward
Over the years, we've seen a lot of so-called JKD instructors teaching with the strong side in the back. This is not necessarily a bad thing. Boxing's set up that way. It's just not JKD. I'm not sure why so many instructors who supposedly teach Bruce Lee's art would teach this when it's so plainly and repeatedly stated in Bruce Lee's own writing that the strong side goes in front: "In this stance, you will attack mostly with the right hand and right foot just as a boxer in his left stance uses mainly his left jab, hook, etc."[3] If you want to debate this point, just watch the man in any of his films. Right side's always, always, always in front.

I realize that some of you out there are true southpaws. In this case, you'll want to construct your stance with the left side forward. But for the purposes of this book, we'll assume that the strong side is the right side. Sorry to all you lefties out there—you'll just have to do the reverse.

The Feet
As we just mentioned, the stance narrowed quite a bit over the years. We'll be taking a look at the stance in its most evolved form, around the time *Game of Death* and *Enter the Dragon* were filmed. Any stills or footage of Bruce during this time would be a good reference.

Your feet should be a little wider than shoulder width apart. If we were to imagine a line that would align you with your target, it would run by your front toe and under the arch of your rear foot. The front toe should form about a 30° angle with the line. Less than that will make it difficult for you to sidestep (Figure 2.1). More than that will impede your movement forward (Figure 2.2).

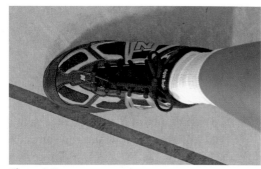

Figure 2.1   **Figure 2.2**

Incorrect foot position of the stance— Too small an angle with the reference line restricts lateral movement (Figure 2.1). Too large of an angle will impede forward movement (Figure 2.2).

Figure 2.3

Ideal foot position— The front foot should form a 30° angle with the reference line. This provides the best balance between lateral and linear movement.

The Left Foot

The left foot, otherwise known as the "engine of the whole fighting machine,"[4] indeed powers your entire fight game. To make sure you're running on all cylinders, keep your left knee bent slightly inward (Figure 2.4). This helps you overcome inertia by preventing any unwanted weight from rolling out the back door.

Next raise the left heel *slightly*. If that heel is too high, you'll have nowhere left to spring from. With the left heel raised, you should feel all of your weight concentrated in the ball of your left foot (Figure 2.5). This is the push-off point. It's this ground reaction force that powers virtually every move in JKD—your punches, kicks, footwork, defensive moves— all of them, even if you aren't covering any distance, originate from that left foot.

Figure 2.4   **Figure 2.5**

Alignment

As we mentioned earlier, an imaginary line should run from the toe of your front foot to the arch of your back foot, and it should be aligned with your target or opponent. If your feet are too far off the line (Figure 2.7), you risk being too open. You are too big of a target, and as we tested in *The Straight Lead*, you will be subject to more jarring upon impact. Similarly, if your feet are aligned toe-to-toe on the line, you will be off balance. Your base of support is too small (Figure 2.6). Footwork will be awkward, and you run the risk of crossing your feet. And, once again, you will not effectively absorb shock on impact.

Figure 2.6
Incorrect foot position—A toe-to-toe position forms too small a base of support. You will always be unbalanced (Figure 2.6). A stance that is too open makes you a larger target, leaving the centerline exposed (Figure 2.7). Both scenarios provide insufficient absorption of forces upon impact.

Figure 2.7

Figure 2.8
Ideal toe-to-arch foot position of the stance—The reference line runs from the front foot toe under the arch of the back foot. This provides the most structural integrity, mobility, and ability to absorb returning forces when throwing a straight lead.

"Small Phasic Bent-Knee"[5]

Both knees should be bent slightly. Doing so allows you to give a little should you end up taking a hit. Springy legs also allow you to regain balance with your footwork. And as we already said, they give potential energy to your punches. In general, your weight should be distributed 50-50 between both legs and you should feel that weight on the medial sides of your legs. If you don't, then you're leaking potential energy to the outside.

Upper Body

To both store potential energy and protect yourself, you'll hunch up a bit with your right shoulder ready to roll up and protect your chin (Figure 2.9). Keep your left hand relaxed and up by the left side of your chin. The upper portion of your right arm should rest on your side, completely relaxed (Figure 2.10). If you can see daylight between your upper arm and your side, then you're putting extra tension on your arm to hold it up (Figure 2.11). This will slow you down! It also takes away all your potential energy and leverage. Just chill and let that arm rest on your side.

Figure 2.9

Ideal hand position—Because the lead hand is not at all extended, you have maximum potential energy. Look for this hand position in the later years of JKD development. You'll see it in Enter the Dragon *and* Game of Death.

Figure 2.10

Figure 2.11

Incorrect hand position—Holding the arm out places too much tension on the deltoid and will slow you down. The partial extension takes away much of your potential energy because you have less room from which to uncoil. You'll see this hand position in the early stages of JKD in the Fighting Method *series.*

Bend your elbow and raise your right hand. Not too high, and not too low. Your hand should be positioned so that all you have to do is shoot straight out, and you'll hit your target. Too low, and you'll have to raise your hand and then shoot out. Too high, and you'll first have to lower your hand before firing.

The following passage was underlined in Bruce Lee's own copy of Thomas Inch's book *Boxing: The Secret of the Knockout:*

> *"For heavy left-hand [lead hand] hitting I do NOT advise holding the left hand well out and high as shown by many professionals in the photographs that we see in boxing magazines. Let the elbow rest upon the hip, and bend the arm so that it has plenty of room in which to move out with the punch."[6]*

It's hard to know exactly when this passage was marked by Bruce, but it would explain the dramatic difference in his upper body position between the *Fighting Method* photos, taken in 1967—with the arm and elbow held out—and the completely relaxed arm position seen in *Game of Death* and *Enter the Dragon* in 1971 and 1973, respectively.

Variations and Other Considerations

Now please keep in mind that this is the stance at its most ideal. This is where you can most effectively utilize your weapons and do so most safely. At closer ranges, you'll need to open up the stance a bit. Also, your alignment constantly shifts as you move with your opponent.

Figure 2.12
Slight opening of the stance for closer ranges.

Obviously, in the heat of battle, things are going to get muddied up. This doesn't mean, though, that technique goes out the window! The more precise you are, the closer you're able to maintain the ideal—all of it gives you that much more advantage over the other guy. It may mean the split-second difference between seizing a target opening or not.

There will also be times when you'll want to keep your right hand down. At closer ranges this is a dangerous proposition, but if you are at a safer distance and are trying to bridge the gap, lowering the lead hand may lure your opponent in. It also allows you to move faster and with greater ease, and it can give you more options that will foul up your opponent. He can now expect a leading straight, hook, or uppercut. It's not the fastest way to throw a straight from the hand-down position, but it's a good way to mix things up and keep the other guy guessing.

CHAPTER THREE

FOOTWORK

"Footwork can beat any attack."

Now that you know how to construct the JKD stance, it's time to learn how to set it in motion. This is, of course, the most obvious purpose of footwork, but it's also *so* much more than a mere transport system. Unfortunately, I hear a lot of instructors minimizing the importance of footwork. They tell their students to mimic the instructor's upper body movement, that the "the feet will just follow." If your "JKD" instructor is telling you this, *run*. Bruce himself wrote, "Having your feet in the correct position serves as a pivot for your entire attack. It balances you properly and lends unseen power to your blows, just as it does in sports like baseball where drive and power seem to come up from the legs." [1]

That footwork gets so little respect in the martial arts is a bit of a conundrum, because it's generally known in other sports that footwork is king. 49er Joe Montana was drafted in 1979 because of his footwork. Andre Agassi attributed the second phase of his career to precise footwork. Football players go to ballet classes. Personal trainers prescribe agility ladder drills. Tennis players run around cones. Even in boxing, it's widely known that footwork is key. It's no fluke that Sugar Ray Leonard modeled his footwork on Bruce Lee,[2] who himself was a cha-cha champion in Hong Kong. It's curious, then, that in the martial arts it's so neglected, even denigrated. It's time for the martial arts to catch up and, once again, this is another instance in which Bruce was ahead of his time.

Footwork is literally the basis of all technique. Bruce never underestimated its importance, declaring, "The quality of a man's technique depends on what he does with his feet." [3] Every punch, every kick, every evasive move starts from the ground up.

But the importance of footwork doesn't end there. Tactically, it is the basis for everything. How you set up your opponent, lull him into a rhythmic pattern, lure him in, and then pounce when the opportunity presents itself—an opportunity made possible via footwork.

Footwork is also the basis for the principles of "defensive offense" and "offensive defense."[4] It should always be your first line of defense. At longer ranges, it's the means by which we maintain a relatively safe distance or what Bruce referred to as the "fighting measure." At closer ranges, it allows you to change your angle relative to your opponent. The flipside to this is that angling off to avoid an attack often results in creating an opportunity for you to counterattack. If you use footwork instead of blocking, this leaves both hands free to fire a counter.

Beginning students, in their rush to start hitting things, often dismiss the elemental importance of footwork. But this would be folly as Bruce wrote repeatedly of its priority status: "Footwork can beat any attack."[5] *Any* attack. For anyone truly interested in Bruce Lee and his art, then, neglecting footwork is not an option.

To summarize, here's a list of some of what makes footwork so fundamentally necessary:

- Movement of your artillery
- Stability both in stationary stance and in mobility
- Technical speed due to place in kinetic chain
- Prevention of overtaxing upper body
- Weight transfer for force production

- Ground reaction force
- Setup's for efficient, naturally flowing combinations
- Maintenance of the fighting measure
- Creation of rhythm and cadence
- Creation of attacking opportunities using time and rhythm
- Makes attacking on the half beat possible
- Creation of angles that provide attacking opportunities
- Evasive techniques at long range
- Evasive techniques at long range that take away angles favorable to opponent
- Longevity due to minimal wear and tear as opposed to blocking
- Leaves both hands free for countering and attacking
- Distance regulator for punching leverage

THE FOUNDATION OF ALL TECHNIQUE

Everything in JKD—and most sports, for that matter—stems from the ground up. Everything. Because of gravity, we are not airborne, so we must generate force to punch, to kick, heck, just to move by using what we call *ground reaction force*. The term is just as it sounds: we push off the ground to generate force. To throw a proper punch, your feet have to move into proper position first. Your feet are attached to your legs, which enable you to transfer the body weight of your trunk. You can't do this if the feet are not positioned properly. Your trunk is attached to your legs, so the legs have to move into the right position to transfer the body weight of your trunk. Usually this involves some kind of hip rotation—this is key to virtually all sports. And, finally, your arm and hand are attached to your trunk.[6, 7] If the trunk is not in the right place at the right time, you'll end up with a pretty unimpressive punch. This sequence of movement from body part to body part is what we call the *kinetic chain*. As you can see, the kinetic chain always starts from the ground up.

One of the key points regarding the kinetic chain is that different segments of the body work together so as not to overtax any single body part. Even if you're not covering any ground, it's still an integral part of any technique. Without the use of your feet, a punch can only occur from the waist up. You will be slower because the arm and waist have to do all the work. And you will certainly not be able to generate any power without the weight transfer from the front to back foot. We call this arm punching.

Similarly, in a defensive move like a bob and weave, if you weave from only the waist without bending your knees and without pushing off from one foot to the other, your upper body is burdened with all the work. You'll be slower and chances are your upper body's going to get tired quicker. But if you get your feet in on the act, you've got the lower body doing at least half the work. You'll be faster, more powerful, and less tired.

Again, this has a lot to do with what Bruce called "unseen power." Even something as imperceptible as a weight shift from one foot to the other makes all the difference.

Every punch requires a specific set of footwork. Proper technique and placement of the feet enables certain punches to set up others, making it possible to efficiently transition from one technique into another.

THE DISTANCE REGULATOR

Another way in which footwork affects your technique is as a distance regulator for you punches, particularly the straight punches. For the straight lead, it's crucial. If you're too close to the target, you'll jam yourself and throw a push, not a punch. Too far away, and, well, you won't even reach the target.

When we cover the straight lead, you'll see that movement from the waist up is almost always the same. Every punch should look identical—the degree of rotation, the contact point, the extension at the elbow. So what accounts for the straight lead's variations in depth and distance covered? Footwork. When it comes to throwing the straight, your back foot is in charge. The depth of your punch—from stinging jab to penetrating power shot—is determined by the rear foot.

In fact, when you fake a lead jab, to be as convincing as possible, you throw it exactly as you would a regular punch. The only difference is that you push off less than you would to reach the target. You intentionally fall short, but only with your feet. The upper body must look just like the real thing.

Footwork, then, isn't just a distance regulator in terms of maintaining the fighting measure. Distance, as controlled by the back foot, also determines the success and efficacy of your punches and fakes.

PRECISION AND THE MOVING PEDESTAL

At its most basic level, footwork is the means by which we get to the target or move away from an attack. In doing so, the most important thing to remember here is that the stance must be maintained as much as possible. Your aim should always be to return to the proper on-guard position. Bruce likened it to a gun turret:

> *"It is essential, therefore, to preserve the balance and poise of the fighting turret carrying your artillery. No matter in what direction or at what speed you move, your aim is to* retain the fundamental stance, *which has been found the most effective for fighting. Let the movable pedestal be as nimble as possible."* [8, 9]

The stance should feel like home. If you are even an inch or two off from the ideal stance, your body should sense that you are off. You shouldn't have to ask yourself, "Is my left foot a few inches too close to the right?" You need to put in enough hours of practice so that your body knows.

Figure 3.1

Figure 3.2

Figure 3.3

Figure 3.4

Imprecise footwork—Failure to advance the back foot (Figure 3.2). Over-advancement of back foot (Figure 3.3).

***Correct maintenance of the stance**—Ted has advanced past the reference line (Figure 3.4) but his stance looks exactly the same as it did before he took that step (Figure 3.1). The back foot is neither lagging behind nor crowding the front foot.*

In practicing footwork, then, the aim should always be to get back to the on-guard position. If your front foot advances 3 inches, your back foot also needs to advance 3 inches. If you sidestep 4 inches to the right with your right foot, you need to sidestep 4 inches to the right with the left foot. When you pivot and swing your back foot to the left, the front foot needs to pivot so that you're still properly aligned with the target. Unfortunately, this kind of precision can only be learned through hours of practice. There's no way around it. It's an easy principle to understand but making your body understand is a matter of muscle memory, which is only acquired by *doing*.

Precision in any JKD movement is what elevates your game. The more precise you are with every motion, the less time you waste making small adjustments. Those tiny corrections may not seem like much, but they will eat you alive. The split second you spent getting yourself into position may be your only window of opportunity. You want to increase the percentage of opportunities you're able to seize.

Obviously there will be times when you deviate from the stance—whenever you throw a punch or kick or move into close quarters. But your aim should always be to return as quickly as possible to the on-guard position because it's the safest place to be as well as the most favorable for launching an attack.

SMALL STEPS

Something that makes precision in maintaining the stance easier is the use of small steps as opposed to larger ones. The reason for this is simple. To remain shifty, it's better to have both feet on the ground. This enables you to spring into action in any direction at any time. If you spend more time than necessary airborne or with one foot off the ground, you don't have nearly as much control over your mobility. You're going to miss out on striking opportunities or get caught with your pants down when an attack comes your way.

There are repeated references to the necessity of small steps throughout Bruce's notes:

> *"Unless there is a tactical reason for acting otherwise, gaining and breaking ground is executed by means of* small and rapid steps. *A correct distribution of weight on both legs will make for perfect balance, enabling the fighter to get off the mark quickly and easily whenever the measure is right for attacks."* [10]

In general, then, each step should really be no more than a few inches in any direction. Even when you push off into a punch, this same principle applies. Even though you are taking advantage of projectile motion, you don't want to spend too much time in the air. Remember that once you're set in projectile motion, once you're in the air, you cannot change directions. You're extremely vulnerable to a counter. The one exception to this small step rule is in the case of retreating. If you need to get out of danger fast, of course, big steps will get you outta there sooner. But you never want to take a large, ungainly stride while advancing.

Small steps also make it possible for you to remain in constant motion without compromising balance and control. The advantage of keeping yourself in motion is especially helpful at close range because there is less inertia to overcome when you do need to make either a defensive or offensive, or, heh, an offensive defensive or defensive offensive move.[11] This kind of constant motion is not movement just for the sake of moving. That's just a waste of energy. No, keeping yourself in motion is only useful at close range when the threat of an attack or the opportunity to launch one is very likely. When you practice footwork, then, think shiftiness, balance, small steps, control, and *stealth*.

USE YOUR DVD PLAYER

We're about to get into the actual footwork arsenal, so there is one very obvious resource that I want you to go to—Bruce Lee himself. I've said it before and I'll say it again and again and again. We can write volumes about technique, but what we're describing is motion, and there are limitations as to what we can tell you in a book. We can describe in great detail all the nuances that we otherwise could only present through hundreds of hours of private instruction. And we can tell you the why's of what we're doing. Both are necessary. But in the end, you cannot only read about technique. This is especially true of footwork. I've a sneaking suspicion that one of the reasons it is so often neglected is that the nuances are incredibly difficult to perceive. To the untrained eye, it's hard to pick up on what separates superior footwork from average. This is where we are fortunate to have Ted Wong's analysis, which is what we'll present here. But to truly benefit from this analysis, you should dig up your Bruce Lee DVD's, use the remote control, and slow everything down frame by frame. See if you can spot all the excellent examples of what we're about to describe.

BEGINNING FOOTWORK

At its most fundamental level, footwork is about moving your artillery, and this can only be done in four directions: advancing, retreating, circling left, and circling right.[12],[13] Of course, like our five punches and four kicks, the variations and applications are endless.

THE FORWARD SHUFFLE/STEP AND SLIDE

In the *Tao* this is referred to as the forward shuffle, but you may also hear Ted Wong refer to it as the step and slide, because, well, that's what you do—you step with one foot, and then you slide up with the other. This is a relaxed form of footwork, what I like to call "stalking footwork." It's the step fighters use to feel each other out. No one's attacking, and no one's rushing to get out of the way.

What distinguishes the forward shuffle from other ways of advancing is that the front foot initiates the movement, not the back (Figure 3.6). You simply pick up your front foot, just enough to get off the ground, land on your heel, and as the rest of your foot settles to the ground, bring the back foot off the ground just enough so that it can advance the same distance as the front foot. Remember to maintain the integrity of the stance at all times.

When you land with the front foot, it's important to land first with the heel, not the toe. This gives you a lot more control over your footwork. A larger base of support gives you more stability. If you land with your toe first, your toe has a lot less surface area than your heel, so your landings will be less stable. The instability caused by placing all your weight at the front of the foot on the less stable toe will require unnecessary braking, making you slower as well.

The "slide" part of the name is a bit of a misnomer. You don't keep either foot in contact with the ground, but they should be raised just enough to clear the floor and still look like you're gliding along.[14] (Figure 3.7)

The step and slide, while the most basic form of footwork, is also tactically the most fundamental. The majority of your footwork time will be spent stepping and sliding to size up your opponent, set him up with patterns, and catch him on the half-beat.

Figure 3.5

Figure 3.6

Figure 3.7

Figure 3.8

Step and slide

THE BACKWARD SHUFFLE/REVERSE STEP AND SLIDE

Just like it sounds—the backward shuffle is the reverse of the forward shuffle. You pick up the rear foot ever so slightly, just enough to clear the floor, and step back a few inches. The front foot follows, again, the same number of inches that the back foot retreated so as to maintain the stance. The reverse step and slide is just as necessary and used just as frequently as its forward counterpart.

The combination of the forward and backward shuffle make maintenance of the fighting measure possible and is the basis for ways of attack like PIA (Progressive Indirect Attack). A variation of this backward/forward shuffle is the tactical step in/step out move. From the *Tao*:

> *"Constant steps forward and back with a carefully regulated length can* conceal a player's intentions *and enable him to lodge himself at the ideal distance for an attack, often as the opponent is off-balance."* [15]

THE QUICK ADVANCE/THE PUSH STEP

The quick advance—often referred to as the push step in Ted Wong's seminars—is, as the name implies, a faster version of the forward shuffle. At least that's what it looks like. The big difference, though, is in how the step is initiated. Remember the forward shuffle starts with the front foot. The quick advance, however, starts with the *rear* foot. To move faster, you need something more to propel you than a falling step. To generate that force, you push off the ground—hence the term **ground reaction force**—with the ball of your left foot.

While the quick advance only looks like a faster version of the step and slide, there is a huge difference, but it's one you must feel instead of watch. Even though it is faster than the step and slide, you still want to remain as close to the ground as possible to maintain control, balance, and stealth. As Bruce noted, "It is not a hop." [16]

THE QUICK RETREAT

You can also push step in reverse. In this case, instead of merely picking up the back foot and stepping backwards, you *push* off the front foot backwards. Because in the stance, your front foot is flat on the ground, you usually will push off the entire front foot—not just the ball of the foot—when you push step backwards.

The quick advance is used when the intensity of a situation turns up. If you are pressing your opponent or if you are being pressed, you may push step forward or backward, respectively.

Shuffle Back

There's another way to quickly retreat and that's by way of shuffling back. From the stance, swing the front leg back as you move your back leg out of the way. The front foot should end up where your back foot was originally, and your rear foot should land in a spot that puts you right back into the stance. This is a form of what we call replacement footwork. One foot "replaces" the other (Figures 3.9–3.11).

The reason the shuffle back is so fast has, once again, to do with gravity. As you swing your leg back, keep your upper body where it is. When you pick up that front leg by swinging it back, you simultaneously move your back foot out of the way. Both feet are momentarily off the ground. You actually fall into the shuffle. When your front foot lands, you should be looking right over it, right over your toes (Figure 3.10). At this point, simply let the back foot settle to the ground so that you end up in, what else, the stance!

This is a great way to avoid kicks, when getting your leg out of the way is priority. It can be accompanied by a downward parry that can deflect a kick and serve as a distance gauge. In all of his films, there is at least one example of Bruce shuffling back to avoid a kick.

The shuffle back can also be used when firing a straight lead as your opponent is advancing. It keeps you at a safer distance from your opponent, and if he's cramping your style and you want to throw a straight lead, you can shuffle back to give you better leverage so your punch isn't reduced to a push.

Figure 3.9
Shuffle back

Figure 3.10

Figure 3.11

Pendulum Step

The pendulum step is just an extension of the shuffle back. Once you've swung the front leg to where the back leg used to be, do not let your back foot touch the ground, and do not let your weight go back with it. Instead, keep your weight up front. All of your weight is over your front foot. At this point swing your back foot forward and move your front foot out of the way. So now your back foot replaces your front foot. Just like the name implies, your legs swing backward and then forward, just like a pendulum.

The first move gets you out of harm's way. The second puts you back in range to throw a counter kick or punch. You'll see Bruce use this one a lot, too, on film.

SIDESTEPPING

You can move your artillery laterally by sidestepping, either as a stalking step and slide or to throw crosses, hooks, and drop shifts. Sidestepping in stalking mode is pretty straightforward. To sidestep right, move your front foot a few inches to the right. Follow up with the left foot the same number of inches to the right so that, as always, you retain the integrity of the stance (Figures 3.12–3.14).

Figure 3.12
Sidestepping right

Figure 3.13

Figure 3.14

To sidestep left, you move the left (rear) foot first and then follow up with the right (front) foot to end up right back in the stance (Figures 3.16–3.18)

This is the fundamental rule of sidestepping: if you're moving right, step first with your right foot (Figures 3.12–3.14). If moving left, the left foot moves first. Never cross your feet.[17, 18]

Figure 3.15

Never cross your feet!—*This is just asking for trouble.*

We've mentioned the idea of cheating inertia in the biomechanics chapter. But there is also reference to it in Bruce Lee's writings on sidestepping: "In order to step in the quickest possible manner, the body should sway over in the direction you are going slightly before the step is made." [19] You don't want to lean past your base of support, because this will put you off balance. But if you want to sidestep quickly to the left, for instance, bend at the waist and lean towards the left boundary of your base of support (Figures 3.16–3.18). The slight offsetting of your center of mass lets you take advantage of gravity's pull. You'll move faster with less effort.

Figure 3.16
Sidestepping left

Figure 3.17

Figure 3.18

Sidestepping is especially useful for dealing with rushers. Instead of meeting them linearly head on or by retreating (and you'll surely get caught if you do this), take the train off the tracks by sidestepping left or right. And as Bruce and Haislet wrote, moving laterally when taking on a rusher opens up countering opportunities for you.[20, 21]

CIRCLING/PIVOTING

Pivoting or circling is a variation of sidestepping. Sometimes moving purely laterally doesn't put you in the best position. The advantage of pivoting is that you can change the angle—sometimes to one that is more advantageous than a sidestep would allow—while staying within range to fire an offensive or a counter.

To circle right, or counterclockwise, pick your right foot off the ground and turn your foot counterclockwise to the desired degree. Use your toe as a pointer. You should set your right foot down at the location where you'll want your stance to be.[22, 23] Keep in mind, then, that your toe does not point directly towards your target because of the 30° angle with our alignment reference line (Figure 3.20). Your right foot should be placed in the position that will align you with the target in the proper stance. You pivot as your foot is *off* the ground. Then you step down. When the right foot comes down, swing the left (rear) leg around so that you are back in the stance and properly aligned with your opponent.

Figure 3.19
Pivoting right

Figure 3.20

To circle left, move your left foot first. Swing your left leg all the way around clockwise to the desired position (Figure 3.22). Once the left foot touches down, pick up your right foot and pivot until you are aligned with the target. Then touch down with your right foot (Figure 3.23).

The pivot isn't limited to turning about a fixed axis either. You can actually take up real estate by stepping and pivoting simultaneously. For example, you can sidestep and pivot right. Move your right foot to the right as you would for a regular sidestep but as you're doing that turn your foot counterclockwise. Anticipate where you'll need to land to align with your opponent. When your right foot touches down, swing that left foot all the way around so you are in the stance and still aligned with the target.

The pivot can be a bit troublesome for beginners. It takes some practice getting used to anticipating how much of a pivot will put you in the right place when you touch down. Don't worry. It's the same as developing a sense of distance.

You learn by doing.

Figure 3.21
Pivoting left

Figure 3.22

Figure 3.23

THE PUSH OFF: THE FOUNDATION OF STRAIGHT PUNCHING

We've just covered the four ways in which you can move your artillery—forward, backward, left, and right. Now it's time to explain how to put that artillery to use. For every punch or kick, there is an accompanying set of footwork. For punching, the most fundamental of these is the push off.

You can think of the push off as the push step to the *n*th degree. Just like the push step, you initiate from the ground reaction force of the ball of your left foot. The difference is one of intensity. You'll find no better description of the magnitude of that intensity than Aldo Nadi's:

> *"Raising the left heel ever so little, you cock the leg ready to pull the trigger and go into action. You take full advantage of one of the mightiest springs in all creation, the arch of the foot, which in the lunge releases its tremendous power through the pressure exerted on the ground by the ball of the foot itself."*[24]

Bruce quoted heavily from this passage in Nadi's book, which is the source of all his spark plug and piston references.[25] And if you watch Bruce, you'll see that while the JKD push off doesn't finish with the same extension as a fencing lunge, it is intended to have the same explosive power.

To obtain maximum power, there are several small things that make huge differences. As with all JKD technique, it starts with the stance. Remember we want to keep that left toe pointed slightly inwards. This helps to keep all of your weight on the medial sides of your legs. When you push off, then, you won't have any weight rolling out the back door. You'll have less inertia to overcome.

The other thing that can minimize inertia is something we talked about in the biomechanics chapter. Without overtaking your base of support, lean slightly forward towards the front boundary of that base. This shifts your center of gravity in the direction you're pushing towards. This is the same thing a sprinter does at the starting block. On the "get set" signal, the sprinter shifts his center of gravity forward and slightly upward. Recall that a raised center of gravity is less stable which is desirable when you are about to set something into motion.

So before you launch into a push off, you'll turn to the right at the waist, which opens up the stance just a hair. To facilitate this hip turn, push up off the left foot ever so slightly, raising your center of gravity. For combative purposes, though, this is a very subtle move and should be imperceptible to your opponent and used only at the last moment before you push off. By raising your center of gravity and shifting your weight towards the front of your support base, you are, in effect, cheating inertia.

Immediately after this shift, of course, you'll push off the ball of your left foot and take off like a rocket. The next problem is the landing. As with all advancing footwork, always, always, always land with the heel of your front foot first and then let the rest of your foot touch down. This is even more important with the push off because you have so much more momentum to control and stop upon landing.

Even with all that power, the small step rule still applies. The push off is a short, explosive launch into a punch. It is not a leap. The longer you stay in the air, the more time your opponent has to avoid or intercept your attack. But the smaller and more controlled your push off is, the better you'll be able to maintain balance upon landing, which makes following up with a combination much easier.

The depth of the push off, of course, may vary. If you are chasing a runner or know that you can pop him with a one shot deal, then you will come in deeper than usual. Just remember to do so only if you can maintain your balance and control. You can develop greater range with your push off by practicing what we call "power footwork." To do this, lower your center of gravity by bending your knees a little more than usual. You wouldn't do this in a fighting situation, but practicing the push off from this position will help you develop the muscle you need to increase your range.

As with all footwork, precision is key and can be especially frustrating with the push off. In the beginning you may find it difficult to land exactly back in the stance because of the increased momentum. In the beginning, you'll want to watch this like a hawk. When you practice, push off. Stop. Check yourself. Are you back in the stance just as you left it? If so, pat yourself on the back. If not, readjust your stance. It's only a matter of muscle memory, but you've got to develop it by consciously taking note of whether or not you're in the proper position. Eventually this will become second nature. Keep at it and just remember that the quality of your straight punches depends on the quality of your push off.

You don't necessarily have to take up any space to push off either. If the target is close, and you can't move forward without jamming yourself, this doesn't mean you skip the push off. Even pushing off in place allows you to take advantage of ground reaction force and projectile motion. Get your body slightly off the ground and you've got a force vector that still moves in two directions—towards the ground and towards the target. Take advantage of this!

An extreme example of the push off in place is Bruce Lee's one-inch punch. If you watch the Long Beach demonstration footage, slow down the DVD and you'll see him push off the ground to power that punch. The footwork may be subtle, but you can see that it allows him to turn his hips, too. Without that push off, imperceptible as it may be, there'd be no way he could generate such power at such close proximity. This is why the left foot is called the "piston of the entire fighting machine."[26] Without the push off, you have no offense.

Figure 3.24

Figure 3.25

Figure 3.26

Figure 3.27

Figure 3.28

The push off—*On paper, the push off looks very much like the step and slide. The difference is that the front foot initiates the step and slide, while the back foot powers the push off. The difference is essentially one of intensity. You will see examples of the push off in all punching techniques throughout the following chapters.*

CHAPTER FOUR

THE STRAIGHT LEAD

The straight lead is not just an approximation of a jab. Effective execution involves very specific sequencing and positioning. This is the case with all punches, but the straight lead is the most difficult to master because as both Bruce Lee and Edwin Haislet observed, hitting straight "is not a natural act." "It is an art," Haislet wrote, "that takes years of study to practice to perfect."[1] For all the reasons Bruce Lee outlined in his own writings, devoting years of study to this punch is necessary to truly understand JKD.

The principles behind straight lead mechanics are the same for all other JKD techniques. We want to maximize force production by maximizing acceleration of the hand or foot at impact. And we want to do so with a minimal amount of motion or deviation from the stance.

Maximization of acceleration is a result of careful sequencing of each body part in the movement. This is what is now referred to as the *kinetic chain*. The important thing to remember here is that Bruce Lee was not just imitating a punch from another art. True, there are elements inspired by both Western fencing and boxing, but it is far too simplistic to say he took a little of boxing and little of fencing and threw them together. Nor was he guessing as to what works. The straight is a brilliant martial arts development based on sound mechanics—science. To perform the straight lead, then, with anything less than the exact sequencing and positioning is not to perform the straight lead at all.

That sequencing is as follows:
1. Cheating Inertia and Drawing In
2. The hand
3. The push-off
4. Hip rotation and shoulder extension
5. Contact with target
6. Landing of front foot
7. Landing of rear foot and hand retraction

Let's go over these points one by one.

CHEATING INERTIA AND CORE STABILIZATION
Before you do anything—before you move the hand, the feet, or your center of gravity—you can help yourself a lot by shifting your body weight forward as we mentioned in both the biomechanics chapter and the section on the push off. To review, remember you can turn your hips so that you open the stance very, very slightly. You do so by raising your left heel (Figure 4.2). It should be to such a small degree that it is imperceptible to your opponent. This shifts your center of gravity up and places it towards the front boundary of your base of support. This is the "slightly forward center of gravity"[2] of which Bruce wrote. Do not overtake that base of support or you will become unbalanced.

This launch needs to be explosive. The faster your push off, the faster you accelerate into the punch, and mass times acceleration equals force—so the more explosive your push off, the more forceful your punch. Keep your left knee pointed inward so inertia is easier to overcome—none of your weight should roll out the back door.

Maintain the integrity of your stance. If you are precise in your footwork, you will never be caught with your feet too wide apart or too close together. If they're too far apart, you have no leverage, nowhere from which to spring into action. And if they're too close together, you lack a stable base from which to spring and also have minimal leverage. Maintain the stance, though, and you will always be ready to get a shot off.

HIP ROTATION AND SHOULDER EXTENSION

In all sports, hip rotation is one of the most important factors in generating force. Whenever you throw a baseball, hit a forehand, swing a golf club, or, yes, throw a punch, hip rotation is key to transferring your body weight. While it is less pronounced with the straight lead than it is for any of our other punches, it can still make or break you. The reason is twofold. One—and we just talked about this—you maximize your power potential by turning your hip towards the target. Stop short, and you won't get the full benefits of hip rotation.

Figure 4.3

Full hip rotation for the straight lead

Figure 4.4

Figure 4.5

Incomplete hip rotation—This will sell your punch short, as you're not getting the benefits of the full range of motion.

The second reason has to do with acceleration. When you launch your body into the air as a projectile, you are subject to air drag and gravity. Think of shooting an arrow. It gets slower before it hits the ground due to air drag. The same happens to you as you push off into the straight lead. To compensate for drag time, turn your hips into the punch right after pushing off the ground. So while your body may be slowing a bit on the way down, your fist is still accelerating because of that hip turn.

As your hip is turning, your shoulder is extending and your fist is shooting out. This obviously also contributes to hand acceleration. Your hips are going to put your shoulders in the right position. The seam of your pants should be facing the target at the end of the punch (Figure 4.8). You'll also notice that this hip turn is part of what makes the straight so safe. You actually become more closed off to your opponent as you throw the punch (Figures 4.6–4.8)

Figure 4.6

Hip rotation and the straight lead

Figure 4.7

Figure 4.8

The important thing to remember is to keep your knees bent. A lot of people mistakenly think that because the straight lead is a forward linear punch, they need to straighten their legs and lean forward into the punch (Figure 4.10). True, you do lean slightly forward with the torso, but we know from our definition of balance that you never want your torso to overtake your knee (Figure 4.9). It's okay to lean a little at the waist, but keep those knees bent and your center of gravity low. The lowered center of gravity ensures a stable foundation for your punch.

Figure 4.9

***Correct extension**—While Ted's weight is towards the front of his base of support, his head and torso do not overtake his front foot.*

Figure 4.10

***Incorrect extension**—Head and torso overtake the base of support resulting in loss of balance, stability, and power.*

SNAPPINESS AT IMPACT

In *The Straight Lead*, I explained the origins and reasons behind the vertical fist and why we use the bottom-three knuckles.[7] We may argue the virtues and disadvantages of this all we want, but its legitimacy as the preferred technique according to Bruce Lee is undisputed. This is illustrated quite clearly in *The Fighting Method*[8] series, in film footage, and in Bruce Lee's own notes.[9]

The main thing to remember regarding impact is that distance is key. This is where footwork makes all the difference. Obviously, if you're too far away from the target, you won't reach it. But if you're too close to the target, you'll jam yourself, and your punch turns into a push. When you do a chest press, you have the most leverage at the last 3 or 4 inches of the movement. The same goes for straight punching.

Your arm and body should be positioned so that at impact, your arm can only extend another 3 or 4 inches past the target. This is a point Bruce certainly emphasized. "All punches," he wrote, "should end with a snap several inches behind the target. Thus, you punch *through* the opponent yet end the punch with a snap."[10]

Though Bruce didn't go into the details of *why* punches should only extend a few inches past the target, the answer can be found in the laws of physics. We talked about this in our discussion of impulse and momentum. If you were to extend your arm and hand for more than 4 inches of contact with the target, you increase your contact time and decrease the force of your punch. This is why it's so important to retract your hand immediately after you've followed through with your punch. The faster you change direction, the less contact time with the target and the more force you generate. This is what Bruce meant by keeping your punches "snappy." So aim to retract the hand faster than you throw the punch.

In a lot of cases, if your hand is moving fast enough and your knuckles are very dense, just tapping your opponent can do damage. 3 to 4 inches of punching depth is just enough. More than that, and you unnecessarily increase impact time and decrease force—that's a push, not a punch.

Figure 4.11

The straight lead at impact—*Photographer Jim Henken did an amazing job of catching me midair at impact. Both feet are a few inches above the ground. I've just made contact and I've judged the distances so that my arm is bent just enough to allow for extension 3–4 inches through the target.*

THE STRAIGHT LEAD 59

FRONT FOOT LANDING

Straight lead footwork might be thought of as combining the best of fencing and boxing. The initial forward and upward portion of the push off clearly comes from the fencing lunge and Nadi's raised left heel. The second half of the push off is the landing, and this comes from Dempsey's book. This is where we take advantage of gravity and "fall" into the punch *downward* and forward.

Dempsey referred to this as the "falling step" and "the gem of straight punching." After you push off, both feet are momentarily off the ground. You are unstable. You're falling. To regain stability, let your front foot touch the ground but *not* before you hit the target. As you fall during the latter half of projectile motion, you are directing force both downward and forward. If your foot lands first, all that good force goes into the ground. What a waste! Instead, take advantage of gravity by hitting the target before hitting the ground.

The main thing to remember about the mechanics of landing is that you want to land heel first. The heel covers more surface area than your toes and is more stable, so land on the heel first, then just let the rest of your foot step down. Watch Bruce and you'll see he lands heel first whenever he pushes off.

This is the first step of what we call the Three Point Landing. Hand hits target. Front foot lands. Back foot lands. We'll come back to the third point, but first we need to discuss retraction of the hand.

HAND RETRACTION

Somewhere between the landing of the front foot and landing of the back foot, you're going to retract the front hand. As you might expect, this is not an arm-only affair. In fact, what initiates retraction of the hand after impact is not the arm, but the hips! Think of everything occurring in reverse order. To throw the punch, the hand moves first and the hips move after. At impact, you're like a fully stretched rubber band. At full extension, first turn your hips in the opposite direction you turned when throwing the punch. This initiates the turn of your shoulders back to the on-guard position, and as your shoulders are turning, relax your arm and let the momentum of your turning torso retract the hand.

The path of your arm needs to be straight as an arrow. Straight in as you throw the punch and straight out back into position. The most common mistake among beginners is dropping the hand. This is caused either by poor technique or fatigue. Dropping the hand wastes energy, slows you down, and leaves you open to counterattacks. It dissipates your power because you end up sliding off the target, increasing contact time with the target resulting in decreased force concentration. If you lower your hand on the way back, then you have to raise it to throw another punch. Throwing effective double and triple jabs won't be much of an option for you. So whenever you throw a straight punch of any kind, think like Haislet who wrote, "The arm must travel a straight line and return in a straight line."[11]

Figure 4.12

Figure 4.13

Figure 4.14

Figure 4.15

Figure 4.16

***Retraction of the hand**—In Figure 4.13 my arm is still fully extended but my hip is already moving. It isn't almost until the hip is back to its starting position that my hand starts to retract (Figure 4.14).*

LANDING OF THE BACK FOOT

Once the front foot touches down, simply let the back foot touch down right after. This time, though, you don't land heel first because you need to keep that back left heel up to maintain springiness and readiness to get the next shot off. Hopefully, your heel-first front foot landing will have already stabilized you.

The most important thing to remember about the third point of your landing is that the back foot only advances as much as the front foot did during the push off. This puts you right back in the stance and ready to fire a double or triple jab.[12]

"THE BACKBONE OF ALL PUNCHING"

We've just gone through the pretty intricate sequence of the straight lead. It's easily the most difficult tool in the JKD arsenal. But Bruce called it "the backbone of all punching in Jeet Kune Do,"[13] "the core of Jeet Kune Do,"[14] and said that "90 percent of all hitting is done with the leading right hand."[15] So it's pretty clear that you cannot really practice JKD without a good straight lead. This will become evident when we discuss application and feinting.

The good news, though, is once you can throw the straight, all other punches in our arsenal are relatively easy. Once you understand the principles behind the lead right and can execute them, the rest is cake.

Figure 4.17

Figure 4.18

Figure 4.19

Figure 4.20

Figure 4.21

Figure 4.22

Straight lead mechanics—*The hand is already well on its way by the time I push off (Figure 4.18). I've already made contact and fully extended the arm by the time my heel just starts to touch down (Figure 4.19). For a complete follow through, I allow for full hip rotation (4.20). As the back foot lands, my hand is already retracting along the same path from which it shot out (Figure 4.21). At the end of the punch I end up precisely back in the stance. My feet are neither too close nor too wide apart (Figure 4.22).*

CHAPTER FIVE

VARIATIONS OF THE STRAIGHT LEAD

There are several other straight punches that are thrown with the lead hand. These include the corkscrew, which is similar to the cross in trajectory; the backfist, which follows a subtle left-to-right path; the drop-shift, a low line lead punch; and the shovel hook, a close relative of the uppercut. Let's take a look at each of these variations.

THE CORKSCREW HOOK

In terms of trajectory, the corkscrew is very much like a mirror image of the left cross. It's a punch thrown with the right hand that is often used when your opponent is to your left. This can either be in close quarters, when angling up at the elbow is necessary to maintain leverage, or when your opponent circles to your left.

Corkscrew Footwork

The trademark footwork that accompanies corkscrew hooks is the pivot step. If your opponent circles to your left, you'll need to move to get him. You could pivot and then throw a straight, but this takes two steps and is much slower. Instead, from the on guard position, shoot your hand out a hair before pivoting counterclockwise.

Maximizing force production for a corkscrew hook starts with, you guessed it, footwork. When you pivot with the front foot, ideally, you want to swing the back leg around so that you end up with your hip pointing towards the target. This does three things. One, it gets more of your body weight into the punch. Two, it puts you right back into the stance and in alignment with your opponent. And, three, it moves you completely out of harm's way, especially when facing a left stancer. In that case, you both attack and move to his outside simultaneously—a pretty ideal situation. As with the straight lead, even though you're pivoting, you want to stick the target before your front foot hits the ground.

Figure 5.1
Starting position from the stance

Figure 5.2
Failure to bring the back foot around—This prevents you from getting your weight into the punch and limits range of motion.

Figure 5.3
Correct pivot with corkscrew—Bringing the back foot around enables you to point your hip towards the target and gives you greater range of motion through the punch.

When you pivot, you can also regulate the distance as well. You can step and pivot at the same time. The amount of real estate you cover will depend on your distance from the target. Sometimes you'll step to the outside and pivot. At other times, you'll come in deep and advance as you pivot (Figure 5.5). Sometimes you'll just pivot in the same spot. In either case, though, be sure to swing that back leg around so you're not out of position for long. You can trace these points and Bruce Lee's own notes on corkscrew footwork directly to Jack Dempsey.[1, 2]

Figure 5.4
Aerial view of corkscrew pivot

Figure 5.5

At close range, the corkscrew changes a bit. You may not always have time or room to pivot. In this case, you throw the punch like you would a cross. The footwork is similar to that of a cross or straight. You still push off the left foot. The distance to the target determines how much ground you'll cover. At really close range, you may not cover any at all, but you must still push off. And while hip motion may be greatly abbreviated, you still rotate your front hip in the direction of the target.

Corkscrew Mechanics

Mechanics for the corkscrew hook are dependent on the accompanying footwork, but there are also some very important upper body mechanics that distinguish it from the straight lead. The most obvious of these tweaks is the palm down hand position. This has to do with our body structure. When you throw a straight lead, the trajectory is just as the name implies, straight ahead. In that case, it is most natural according to Dempsey's Power Line, to throw from the shoulder with a vertical fist.

The corkscrew is different. Your target is to your left so the trajectory of the punch is much like a cross. You are crossing the center line and starting from your right but ending up to your left. Because of this crossing over effect, the best way to throw a corkscrew is with the palm down. Again, it has to do with our body structure. You don't have the benefit of the same hip rotation as the straight lead here, but the corkscrew has its own benefits. Turning the hand over gives you some additional torque. Ideally, you'll want to turn the hand over so from your opponent's point of view, your pinky knuckle is at 10 o'clock and your index knuckle is at 4 o'clock (Figure 5.6).

The timing of when you turn the hand over is also very important. For a long -range corkscrew, the hand starts out very much like a straight lead. Once it is halfway out of the gate, though, turn the hand over. This keeps you deceptive and adds acceleration to the end of your punch.

Figure 5.6
Palm-down position

Figure 5.7
Angling up in close quarters

When throwing a corkscrew in very close quarters, though, this changes. With the straight lead, remember you have to judge the distance carefully to maximize leverage. You can't be too far or too close to the target—just enough to have 3–4 inches of follow through. Well, the beauty of the corkscrew is it allows for some fudging with the distance. If you're too close, you can lift the elbow up to give you leverage and avoid jamming yourself. At extremely close range, the elbow comes up fast and first, giving your punch a downward angle and additional torque (Figure 5.7)

There is a continuum of angles for the corkscrew. At one end of the spectrum is a punch that very closely resembles the straight lead (Figure 5.8) and is used at medium range. At the other end is a very tight, bent elbow, high-line hook that is essentially a hook thrown with the palm down (Figure 5.10). And, of course, there is everything in between these two extremes, which makes the corkscrew a very versatile punch at medium and close ranges.

Figure 5.8
Corkscrew continuum

Figure 5.9

Figure 5.10

Corkscrew Applications

The corkscrew is especially useful when your target is to your left or when your opponent is circling to your left. It is especially useful against left stancers because the pivot step moves you to their outside. You're fully protected and have a shot at an opening.

Because of this, it is a great counter against left stancers when they throw left leads or as Bruce noted whenever your opponent moves to your left as with a left cross thrown by a right stancer or a right thrown by a left stancer.[3, 4]

In close quarters, the corkscrew can also get to places that other punches just can't, much like an overhand cross. Even if your opponent's hands are up or he throws a punch with his left, he can still be very vulnerable to a corkscrew to either side of his head as you shoot over his arm and downward towards his head.[5, 6]

THE BACKFIST

The backfist, unlike the hook, is a punch that actually moves to your outside from left to right. While it does not generate as much power as other punches, it is probably the fastest punch in our arsenal due to its relaxed, whip-like motion. Should you be caught with your lead hand slightly off center to your left (Figure 5.11) or if your hand is held low and to the left, the backfist is your fastest option. It's also useful if you find your opponent moving to your right.

Backfist Mechanics and Footwork

The mechanics of the backfist are almost the same as with the straight. The only difference here is the trajectory of the hand, which instead of shooting straight out moves from left to right (Figures 5.11–5.13).

The impact surface should be the outside of your bottom three knuckles. You can also vary this by starting with a traditional backfist but finishing the punch by landing with the same surface that you would use for a regular straight lead.

Because of its potential for speed, the same motion of a backfist is often combined with a finger jab. Even though you may not have the leverage of other punches, the speed of the hand means minimal contact with either knuckles or fingers can cause considerable damage.

Figure 5.11

Corkscrew mechanics

Figure 5.12

Figure 5.13

VARIATIONS OF THE STRAIGHT LEAD **67**

A TRIO OF STRAIGHT PUNCHES

The backfist, straight lead, and corkscrew hook can be thought of as a set of punches each of which covers a particular range: left to right, straight ahead, and right to left, respectively. This can be a very effective combination that is a variation of a triple jab. From the stance, with the lead hand slightly to your left, throw the backfist, which moves from left to a target slightly to your right. Retract and throw a straight lead straight ahead. Retract and throw a corkscrew at a target slightly to your left by pivoting to your right. This combination not only has all the advantages of throwing triple leads, but the circling motion to the right keeps you mobile and elusive.

THE SHOVEL HOOK

The shovel hook is our low-line straight punch. Though it's called a hook, it is straight in its trajectory. The low-line arcing counterpart of the shovel hook is the uppercut. While the uppercut is mainly vertical with an arcing component, the shovel moves forward, upward, and straight.

Shovel Hook Mechanics

When you shovel hook, you're usually coming out of a duck, slip, or curving step to the right. The punch starts with the palm of your right hand turned up and your elbow in. This is key. You'll see multiple references to this in Dempsey's book and the *Tao*.[7] This actually makes throwing the shovel hook easy. You start out with your right elbow on your hip with your palm up. From there you simply shoot straight out.

In his descriptions of the shovel hook, you'll see that Bruce Lee repeatedly refers to "shoulder hunch," "shoveling hunch," "hip hunch," and "hip whirl." Since you usually throw the shovel hook as you're coming out of an evasive move like a duck or slip, you're usually in a crouch with bent knees and your hips turned slightly clockwise. You are in a bit of a coil with a whole lot of potential energy ready to be released (Figure 5.15).

When you throw the shovel hook, as with other straight punches, the hand moves slightly first, and then you push off with the left foot. There's your "upward surge." At the same time you're pushing upward, you uncoil at the hips counterclockwise. Using the old hip rule as our guide, point your hip towards the target. In the case of the shovel hook, this is accomplished by moving your front hip forward and counterclockwise out of that coil (Figure 5.16). The best description of this comes out of the *Tao*, which in turn, comes directly from Jack Dempsey:[8]

> *"Pull your right elbow in and press it firmly against the front edge of your hip bone. Turn your half-opened right hand up slightly so that your palm is partially facing the ceiling. Your palm should slant at an angle of about 45 degrees with the floor and ceiling. Meanwhile, keep your left guard in normal position. Now, without moving your feet, suddenly whirl your body to your left in such fashion that your right hip comes up with a circling, shoveling hunch that sends your exploding right fist solidly into the target about solar plexus high. The slanting angle of your right hand permits you to land solidly with your striking knuckles. Make certain you have no tension in your elbow, shoulder or legs until the whirl is started from your normal position. More important, make certain that your hand is at the 45-degree angle and your hip comes up in a vigorous shoveling hunch."* [9, 10]

We didn't talk too much about the footwork accompanying the shovel punch. It's the same push off that you would use with a straight lead or corkscrew. You can pivot and throw the shovel, which will put you at an advantageous angle to a left stancer's outside—ideal for throwing kidney shots. In close quarters, you may not even cover any real estate at all. You would still push off, though. You just may not take up any space to do it. Ideally, you'd also hit the target first and then land the front foot a split second after.

Figure 5.14

Figure 5.15

Figure 5.16

Application

The shovel hook is analogous to the straight lead. At longer ranges, the straight, as we've mentioned, will beat any hooking punch simply because the fastest way from Point A to Point B is a straight line. The same goes for fighting at close range. The shovel hook is especially helpful because the tendency of most fighters here is to throw hooks. You can beat them to the, er, punch by throwing short, tight, and *straight* shovel hooks. As Dempsey wrote, this keeps you "inside the attack of bobbing weavers, most of whom hook from the outside."[11, 12] This is where the elbows-in principle is so important. Being able to throw a punch with those elbows in keeps you well protected (Figure 5.17). You don't take the same chances opening up as you would by throwing a hook.

Figure 5.17
Application of shovel hook

Figure 5.18
The drop shift

The drop shift is another low-line straight punch that can be thrown with either the rear or front hand. In the case of the front hand, it's usually used against a right stancer. It's a very safe punch to throw because you change both your height and angle.

DROP SHIFT MECHANICS

You can push off and move forward with a drop shift. Or you can sidestep to the left by pushing off with your right foot and moving left as you throw the punch.[13] And you can also throw a combination of the two by pushing off at a diagonal angle towards your left. If you do angle to the left, it places you to the outside of a right stancer—again, very safe.

Because you're changing the angle, due to our body structure, you turn the hand over and throw the drop shift palm down. Once again, you'll want to land the punch before the first foot hits the ground. Whether you're pushing off straight ahead or sidestepping, you want to get your body weight into the punch. To do this, you can't be lazy. Drop your center of gravity down by bending your knees (Figure 5.18). You should be at eye level with your hand. And as always, the bottom three knuckles form your striking surface.

Application

The drop shift is a great tool to vary your height and angle and keep your opponent guessing. It is especially useful for setting up and capitalizing on feints and fakes. You can now fake low and go high (Figures 5.19 and 5.20). Or fake high and send a drop shift to the solar plexus (Figures 5.21 and 5.22). Being able to throw low-line shots keeps your opponent guessing and opens up targets.

Figure 5.19

Figure 5.20

Figure 5.21
Drop shift applications

Figure 5.22

CHAPTER SIX

THE REAR CROSS

While the straight lead may be the cornerstone of Jeet Kune Do, you need a good rear cross to be a "two-handed" fighter. Traditionally in boxing, the rear hand is considered your "heavy artillery" for two reasons. First, the position of the hand requires a greater distance to the target, so more momentum goes into this punch. And, two, the mechanics of the rear cross allow for a greater rotational range at the waist. For reasons already explained, Bruce Lee chose to put the strong side up front, but with the mechanical advantages of the rear cross, the non-dominant hand should be able to generate just as much force as the lead.

The main concern regarding the rear cross is that it deviates from the stance more than any other punch in the JKD arsenal. When throwing it, you actually expose the centerline, which is always risky business. Because of this, the cross must be delivered in a way that protects you from counters, and it must always be in the back of your mind that if you miss, you'll be ready to duck or get out of the way.

If you are fighting someone whose lead is the same as yours, you will most likely not want to start off with the cross, because there is too much of a gap to bridge. Instead, work your way in with the lead hand and follow up with the cross. Conversely, the cross is a great lead-off punch when fighting someone whose stance doesn't match yours.

MECHANICS OF THE CROSS

Hand Before Foot

Because the cross is essentially a straight punch, the hand should initiate the punch. Hand Before Foot is especially important for the cross, because the rear hand has further distance to travel to the target than your front hand. Of the left cross, Bruce Lee wrote the following:

The rear left cross is difficult to use because:

1. The fundamental position has the right side forward and therefore the left hand has farther to travel.

2. Likewise, the use of the left hand will present an opening for your opponent if you miss.

"Practice to minimize the above two points," Bruce wrote, "thus perfecting the left cross—non-telegraphic starting, quick recovery."[1]

As with any punch, be as non-telegraphic as possible. When you see your opening, shoot in as straight and cleanly as you can right from the stance. No winding up, no adjustments, no drawing the hand back. Give your opponent *nothing*.

Footwork

Because of the dangerous nature of the cross, it's imperative that your footwork be precise. If you're sloppy with your feet, you won't generate much power or speed, you'll be out of position to throw a follow-up shot, and worse, you won't be able to avoid a counter if you miss. So let's start our explanation of this punch from the ground up.[2]

Just as you would for the straight lead, you'll use the push off to launch your entire body weight into the punch. Remember the three ways to direct force—linear, vertical, and rotational. The rear cross and its relative, the straight rear thrust, are very much like the straight lead in that they are punches with linear trajectories. However, as is the case with the straight lead, punches with the rear hand also depend on vertical and rotational movement.

The fundamental footwork for the cross is the push off. The three-point landing applies here as well. The cross differs from the straight lead because you must deviate significantly from the stance. Recall the reference line we used to explain the JKD stance. The cross, unlike the straight lead, actually requires you to step off that line. You will push off from the stance, but you will land with your right foot to the right of the line (Figure 6.2). This allows you to open up the stance, thereby giving you a fuller range of motion to rotate your left hip.

Figure 6.1
Rear cross footwork

Figure 6.2

Remember that you always want to move the hip on the side of your punching or kicking hand or leg towards the target. So by pushing off and ending up in a position that is open, you'll be able to move that left hip all the way around. If it simply points straight ahead, your motion will be restricted and you won't get the benefits of a full rotation.

Now that you know where the front foot goes, don't forget that back foot. This is a common mistake that beginners make. After the push-off they will often land correctly with the front foot but let the back foot linger behind. If you do this, you're only operating at half wattage. If you fail to move the back foot at all, then you're not getting all of your body weight behind the punch. And if you never get off the ground, then you can't take advantage of directing all of that gravitational force towards the target.

Even worse, allowing that back foot to lag behind leaves it over extended. This restricts your next move. There's nowhere left to go. If you want to throw another punch, you're hopelessly out of position to throw anything—a straight, a cross, a hook. All of these require some "give" in that left leg so you have somewhere from which to spring. If you leave the back leg behind, the spring is already stretched out, and there goes your leverage for the next shot.

For maximum hip rotation, your back foot should point in the same direction as the front foot. You'll want to land with both toes pointing 30–45° (Figure 6.4) outward to the right. If you place the front foot outwards at 45° but your back foot is still pointing straight ahead your hip rotation will be restricted. At close range, you may not even need to take up any real estate. In that case, the footwork is less of a push off and more of a pivot off the back foot. Whether you are pushing off or pivoting, you transfer your weight from the left to right leg, resulting in something close to a 30/70 distribution.[3, 4]

Figure 6.3   **Figure 6.4**

Hip rotation and the cross—*Figure 6.3 is more like a rear straight, which is used if your opponent's on the defensive and you have to chase him. For better power and a bit more elusiveness, you'll want to employ the footwork in Figure 6.4. This gives you more room to rotate your hip and consequently throw more of your weight into the shot.*

Impact

Hand position for the rear cross is very different from that of the straight lead. While keeping that left elbow in close, when your hand is about a third of the way out, start to turn your fist over (Figure 6.7). Because of the open structure of the stance, your shoulders are positioned more squarely to the target and you will generate more power by turning the hand over. The point of impact still consists of the bottom three knuckles. It's ideal to actually turn the hand over at an angle. To your opponent, this would look like your pinky knuckle is at about 2 o'clock and your index knuckle is at 8 o'clock (Figure 6.10). From your point of view, this looks like 10 o'clock and 4 o'clock.

Even though the hook is largely a rotational technique, you can still integrate ground reaction force. Here, both of my feet are actually off ground, giving me extra power and torque.

CHAPTER SEVEN

THE HOOK

THE PUNCHING CONTINUUM

We're going to make a sharp departure from straight punching now and take a look at the arcing punches, which include hooks and uppercuts. But before we do that, keep in mind that between these two extremes is a continuum of punches that covers everything in between.

At the bottom of this continuum is the uppercut, a vertical punch (Figure 7.1). Between the upper-cut and hook is a whole range of punches including shovel hooks and what Ted Wong calls the Sling 45 (Figure 7.2 and 7.3). These are punches that are neither purely vertical uppercuts nor purely lateral hooks.

Similarly, there is an entire range of punches that fall between hooks and straight leads. The hook progresses from mid-range height (Figure 7.5) to high hooks, from high hooks to palm down hooks (Figure 7.6), from palm down hooks to sharply angled corkscrew hooks, and then to straighter corkscrew hooks (Figure 7.7), and finally, to straight leads (Figure 7.8).

While other arts have many techniques and a lot of terminology for those techniques, we JKD practitioners like to say we only really have about 5 or 6 punches. But if you know those punches inside and out, the reasoning behind the mechanics, and when to best use them, you actually have an infinite number of possibilities along that continuum. The adjustments (i.e. palm down vs. vertical fist, elbow angle, degree of angularity) depend on distance to the target and/or target height.

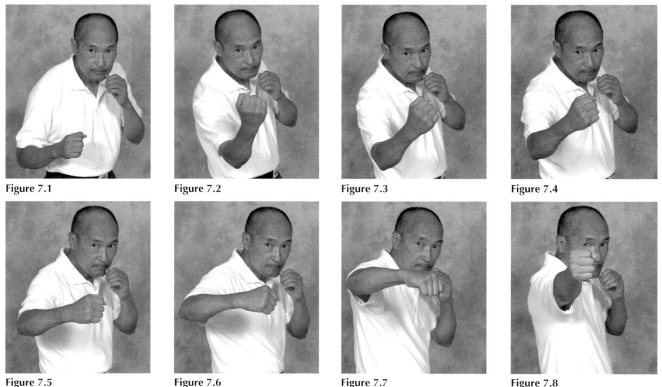

Figure 7.1 **Figure 7.2** **Figure 7.3** **Figure 7.4**

Figure 7.5 **Figure 7.6** **Figure 7.7** **Figure 7.8**

The punching continuum: from arcing uppercut to straight lead

Figure 7.13

Figure 7.14

Figure 7.15

Figure 7.16

Figure 7.17

Sidestepping into a hook—*I weave right (Figure 7.14), and before my left foot lands, I push off to the left (Figure 7.15) as I throw a right hook (Figure 7.16). If the camera had picked up a frame earlier, you would see that I land the target before the right foot lands. This allows me to take advantage of force generated by my body weight and gravity. Upon follow through my right hip is pointing directly at the target (Figure 7.17).*

The side step, then, not only serves a defensive purpose by keeping you elusive in bobbing and weaving, but it also puts you in a better position to throw close range punches by allowing you to put your entire body weight behind them.[5]

Pivoting or Curving Step

A pivot or curving step can get you out of the way at close range. And as you move out of the way, you're also moving to your opponent's outside, giving you a shot at the body or the head. For the body, you'll use the pivot step to put you in position to throw a hook, often to the kidney.

To throw a right hook, pivot right (counterclockwise). To throw a left hook, pivot left (clockwise). This could temporarily have you in a stance with the weaker side forward, which allows you to load up with the right hand in the back. Following up with a left hook conveniently puts you right back into strong side forward.

In either case, learning to throw a hook while pivoting is a bit tricky and may not flow as naturally as side stepping or shifting the weight on to the back foot. When using the curving step, you'll often be moving forward towards the target (Figure 7.19). The step forward can be anywhere between a step and a push off. If you push off, of course, this only adds to the force you can generate. As with the straight lead, it's ideal to make contact with the target before your front foot hits the ground.

Figure 7.18
Step forward with pivot and hook

Figure 7.19

The most important thing to remember when you pivot or curve is that you must bring the back leg around to: 1) put you back into the proper stance and in line with the target and 2) make sure your center of mass turns with you completely into the punch. If you neglect to swing the rear leg around, you are not only out of position, but you are also preventing full rotation and movement of your body weight towards the target.

Figure 7.25   **Figure 7.26**

***Shoulder catch**—The hip turns but the shoulder stays put. This hip turn always initiates the hook.*

There are a few things you can do to get used to feeling that catch on the shoulder. First, you can put your fist against a wall as if you are going to throw a hook. Keep your fist on the wall and turn your hips toward the wall counterclockwise. That tension on your shoulder is what you should feel at impact when throwing a hook. You should not initiate movement of the arm until you feel that catch. To get the idea of how the hips, shoulder, and arm move together, hold a broomstick or some kind of pole on your shoulders and just twist from left to right. This will give you the feeling of the torso and arm moving as one. The most important thing to remember about the hook is that the arm never moves independently of the torso. Think of a door swinging on its hinges to help you visualize this.

Figure 7.27

Maintain the potential strain energy on your shoulder to the point of impact and through the target.

To practice the timing between the hips and shoulder try this: stand with your feet and lower body in the stance but with both arms completely relaxed by your sides. Turn as you would to throw a hook but still with both arms completely limp. Notice how your hips will rotate to a certain degree before your completely relaxed arm eventually follows. That is exactly the kind of timing you are looking for when you throw a hook.

The speed—and force—of the hook is determined by the rate at which you can turn your torso. Of course, minimization of all extraneous motion will help increase your speed, and keeping the technique "tight" will also increase your speed. Think of figure skaters and how much faster they turn as they bring their arms and legs in close. Of course, since the hook is mostly a close-range weapon, keeping it tight is a protective measure as well.[8, 9]

Impact

You can certainly throw hooks palm down, but it seems that Bruce was partial to the vertical fist hook.[10] At impact, your lead hip and fist should be in line with the target. And, of course, your shoulder should be at full extension for maximum leverage.

The most common problem with the hook tends to be with the trajectory of the hand. At one end of the spectrum, I see students arc too much and slide off the focus mitt without penetrating the target (Figures 7.29–7.31).

Figure 7.29

Figure 7.30

Figure 7.31

Failure to hit through the target—Too little time in contact with the target results in a mere skidding off the focus mitt.

At the other extreme are those who throw the hook like a straight punch and end up shortchanging their power because they do not finish their rotation. The result is a kind of weak pushing effect (Figures 7.32–7.34).

Figure 7.32

Figure 7.33

Figure 7.34

Failure to hook—*There is no hooking motion here. The straight trajectory of the hand allows for too much contact time with the target, making this an innocuous push with no hip behind it.*

The reason for this pushing effect has to do with impulse and contact time. Unlike straight punches, in which you throw out the hand and then snap back at full extension, the hook is not a straight out/straight in motion. From our study of impulse, remember that the time during which your hand has contact with the pad determines force. So how do we obtain snap with the hook? It lies somewhere between an arc and a straight punch.

At impact, you move straight through the target for about 4 or 5 inches. So for a fraction of a second the hand does travel on a straight trajectory. To minimize impact time, though, after those 4 or 5 inches, you continue your arcing motion. This enables you to rotate completely and at full speed. After you've hit through the target, your hand will move away from the pad in an almost tearing motion, which gives the punch a little extra kick at the end. Against a real person, this will only increase the damage done as you might take some skin with you.

A good way to practice this tearing motion is to work on the heavy bag. When you a throw a lead hook, as you tear away from it, the bag should rotate in the same direction right after impact. If you are hitting straight through, the bag won't rotate.

Figure 7.35

Figure 7.36

Figure 7.37

Figure 7.38

Figure 7.39

Figure 7.40

Figure 7.41

***Hook mechanics and proper follow-through**—First I turn my lead hip and feel the catch on my shoulder (Figure 7.36). I maintain this tension throughout contact (Figure 7.37) punching 3–4 inches through the target (Figure 7.38). Not until after I've punched through those few inches do I begin the tearing motion (Figure 7.39). As I come off the pad (Figure 7.40) my hand overtakes the hip and follows through until my hand comes to rest by my midsection.*

Follow Through

That circular motion off the focus mitt not only keeps your hook snappy by cutting impact time, but it also enables you to follow through (Figures 7.35–7.41). You can tell if you've followed through correctly because your arm will naturally circle back right around your midsection. If you finish out in front of you, then you are punching too straight (Figures 7.32–7.34) and are finishing too far away from your body. At this point, your hand must overtake your hip and you lose all leverage. And because you are moving forward with the punch, you never get to fully rotate which also minimizes force.

VARIATIONS OF THE HOOK

Oh, where to begin! As Ted always says, "Throwing hooks is like cooking eggs." There are so many ways to do it. There's your regular lateral, vertical fist hook. Or you can throw that same hook palm down. With just a slightly straighter trajectory, that high, palm-down hook can turn into a tight corkscrew. At longer ranges, that tight corkscrew straightens out to become a long-range corkscrew.

You can also throw low line hooks. You can give those low hooks a slight upward trajectory. From there, if you straighten out the punch slightly, you've got a shovel hook. There are also varying vertical degrees at which you can throw shovel hooks. Eventually, you'll end up with a purely vertical punch. This is known as the uppercut, which in some cases, can be thought of as a vertical hook.

Hybrid Hook Punches

You can also combine hooks with other punches to gain momentum for added power and to fake out your opponents. Ted has named one of these punches the Sling 45. You start out throwing an uppercut with your palm up (Figures 7.42–7.44). When your hand is halfway out, change the trajectory of your hand and end the punch as a lateral hook (Figure 7.46). By combining a vertical force with a rotational one, you can potentially end up with greater force production than by throwing a purely lateral hook.

Figure 7.42
Sling 45

Figure 7.43

Figure 7.44

Figure 7.45

Figure 7.46

Another hybrid punch would be the combination of a hook and corkscrew. You'll start the first half of the punch with a horizontal hook (Figure 7.48). Halfway out, raise the elbow, turn the palm over (Figure 7.49) and end with a corkscrew (Figure 7.50). This can be an incredibly powerful punch, especially if you give the corkscrew portion a little downward torque. Once again, giving a punch an extra direction of force gives you even more power than if you'd thrown a regular corkscrew.

Figure 7.47

Hook-corkscrew hybrid

Figure 7.48

Figure 7.49

Figure 7.50

Of course, starting out with one punch and ending as another has the additional benefit of faking out the opposition. If your opponent falls for the initial hooking motion, he won't expect a corkscrew to the head. Or if he's guarding against an uppercut, he's looking out for his chin, and not a heavy body shot.

Loose Hooks and Distance

While the hook is mainly a close range weapon, in some situations you can actually lead off an attack with a longer-range, "loose hook." This is best used as a counter to a straight punch as you time your opponent moving in, but on occasion, you can use it to initiate an attack if you've judged the distance and timing just right (Figures 7.51–7.54). The loose hook necessitates a straightening of the arm which means you'll compromise both power and speed, but if you land the target forcefully—especially as your opponent is moving in on you—does it really matter?

Figure 7.51

Figure 7.52

Figure 7.53

Figure 7.54

Loose hook—*To counter a jab, step back and lower the hand (Figure 7.52). As your opponent retracts the jab (Figure 7.53) straighten your arm a bit and move in with a loose, long-range hook.*

The uppercut's main source of power is ground reaction force. Here, both of my feet are virtually off the ground giving the punch vertical upward force.

CHAPTER EIGHT

THE UPPERCUT

The uppercut is a logical extension of the hook. As we mentioned, it can fall on our punch continuum between a purely vertical punch and a vertical punch with rotational characteristics of the hook. Like the hook, it is used for infighting. In combinations, the uppercut can easily be interchanged with hooks.

FOOTWORK

A lot of people don't think of footwork as being at all involved in throwing the uppercut, because you don't cover any distance. You don't take up much real estate. This is ironic, though, because the majority of the uppercut's power comes from a vertical push off (see opposite page).

Figure 8.1

Figure 8.2

Figure 8.3

Figure 8.4

Uppercutting and Pivoting—*As with the hook, the hip moves ahead of the hand (Figure 8.1) up until the point of contact (Figure 8.2). The crouched position allows me to uncoil fully into the punch. The pivot puts my feet into a position that allows for additional rotation and power.*

You often throw uppercuts when you are coming out of a crouch, either following a cross, slipping a punch, or coming out of a duck or weave. It is, therefore, likely that you have opened up the stance a bit and that your weight is slightly shifted towards the front foot. The uppercut is thrown from the ground up. As you push up and straighten your knees, you transfer your weight from the front foot to the back foot from about a 60/40 to 40/60 distribution. This is addressed in the *Tao* in a passage taken directly from Thomas Inch:

> *"A short uppercut is an effective one. Keep your legs bent before striking; straighten them suddenly as you send the punch in. Get up on your toes and lean back a little as the blow lands, dropping more weight on the left leg when using the right and more on the right leg when using the left."*[1, 2]

Just as you would with the straight lead, you are using ground reaction force to propel your body into the shot, but in this case the direction is upwards. This is basically the push off in place. You are not taking up any real estate, but you still push off with all the intensity as you would with a straight lead. The only difference is that it is directed vertically and not linearly.

Because the uppercut is a close-range weapon, you'll sometimes want to combine the uppercut with a pivot step as you would with a hook. At close range, angling off is the best way to stay elusive and within striking distance.

UPPERCUT MECHANICS: SHOOT FROM THE HIP

The uppercut is a logical extension of the hook, because the mechanics are very similar. You initiate the punch by jerking your front hip upwards towards the target (Figure 8.6). You will feel a catch on your shoulder similar to the one you would feel when throwing a hook. Once again, for maximum leverage, you never want to let the hand overtake the hip, as this is the very definition of arm punching. To get your whole body into the uppercut, then, you need to give your hip a head start. That slight catch on your shoulder means you are fully extended and have maximum leverage. Stretch that rubber band to its limit then let it go. When you're at full extension, the arm has no choice but to move upward with the body.

Because the uppercut is a close-range tool, one of the most important things to remember is to keep it tight by minimizing any extraneous motion. An easy way to ensure this is to keep the elbow right there by your hip (Figure 8.6). Bend at the elbow at a 45 to 90° angle. The arm should be completely relaxed. Do not deviate from this position until after impact. The core initiates the punch and does all the work. The hand is merely along for the ride.

Figure 8.5
Uppercut Mechanics

Figure 8.6

Figure 8.7

IMPACT

The trajectory of an uppercut may vary from a more linear, straight-up direction to the same curving, tearing motion of the hook that we discussed earlier. The most common intended target of the uppercut is, of course, your opponent's chin. You can throw the punch straight up and into the chin, which is a more linear punch.[3] Or for an added pulling action, as we talked about in the chapter on hooking, you can punch straight through the target for 4–6 inches and then curve and tear off the target.

Figure 8.8

Figure 8.9

Figure 8.10

Figure 8.11

Figure 8.12

***Uppercut Follow Through**—I punch through the target 4–6 inches (Figure 8.10) before I start to leave the target (Figure 8.11). Like the hook, the uppercut ends with a hooking, tearing off follow-through (Figure 8.12).*

THE REAR UPPERCUT

When throwing a rear uppercut, you usually begin with a weight distribution that is opposite to that of the lead uppercut—about 60% in the back foot and 40% in the front. As you move into the punch, you will transfer your weight to 60% in the front and 40% in the back. Our good ol' hip pointer rule applies here as well. The hip on the same side as the weapon you are using is your pointer. So if you throw a left (rear) uppercut, move the left hip towards the target[4] (Figure 8.14).

Like the rear cross, the left uppercut has more potential for power because the hand has a greater distance to travel and, therefore, more momentum. You also have the added benefit of having more room to rotate.

When squaring off with left stancers, the rear uppercut can be very effective when combined with a side step to the right. This move can be interchanged with a rear hook using the same footwork. The idea is that as you are firing a shot, you are also moving to your opponent's outside, keeping you slippery-elusive while creating openings for attack. You can only use the rear uppercut, of course, when you've bridged the gap or your opponent has done it for you. The uppercut is already a close-range weapon. Couple that with the fact that you are using the rear hand, and you've got quite a bit of distance to cover. In the *Tao*, Bruce suggests attack by drawing (ABD) and then stepping in with the rear uppercut.[5]

Figure 8.13
Rear uppercut mechanics

Figure 8.14

Figure 8.15

STREAMLINING THE UPPERCUT:
"THE EFFECTIVE UPPERCUT IS THE SHORT ONE"[6]

When you're in close, you don't have a lot of room to work with, and you need to be fast. To further minimize your movement, you may need to decrease the upward force generated by straightening the legs. While the legs and feet are always involved, in this case, you straighten your legs only slightly and remain in more of a crouch. To compensate for the power you are sacrificing, the uppercut now becomes more rotational (Figures 8.18 and 8.19). When I worked the pads with boxing trainer Freddie Roach, this is how he defined the uppercut. There's more twisting at the waist and less vertical legwork. In JKD terminology, we'd call this a combination of a shovel hook and uppercut. Same punch, different nomenclature. When performed correctly, it's a very, very tight punch—excellent for close quarters.

Figure 8.16
Vertical uppercut

Figure 8.17

Figure 8.18
Uppercut with rotational trajectory

Figure 8.19

CHAPTER NINE

EVASION

J ust as Bruce often referred to the principle of "offensive defense," use of the word "evasion" reminds us that evasive techniques serve the purpose of avoiding a blow. Keep in mind, though, anytime your opponent launches an offensive, he has committed to some kind of action and is vulnerable to a counter attack. The line between offense and defense is often a blurry one. For example, if your opponent throws a hook, you counter with a straight knowing that a straight punch will beat an arcing one every time. The straight serves a dual defensive and offensive purpose. In this chapter we'll be explaining evasive maneuvers. Just remember to always, always look for an opening for a counter when you employ them.

Here are a few principles that govern all evasive techniques:

- **The head moves first**—The first objective is to get out of harm's way, and usually people are gunning for your melon. The head—which really moves as one with the torso—moves slightly first, and is then followed by the feet. This is similar to the idea of hand before foot. Let the feet catch up.

- **Balance**—A lot of students find themselves off balance when practicing evasion because they let their center of gravity overtake the base of support defined by their feet. With any lateral movement—weaving, bobbing, or slipping—move only as wide as your feet are set. In general, this means that if you were to look straight down during any evasion, you should be seeing no further than your own knee. If you're looking down on a spot to the outside of your knee or foot, then you've moved too far. Always keep your feet under you.

- **Keep your center of gravity low**—This goes along with the idea of balance. The higher your center of gravity, the less stable you are. If your center of gravity is too high, you're not bending enough at the knees. Plus you're a bigger target.

- **Don't forget footwork**—This is always the first line of defense in and of itself. But even though a lot of defensive moves don't require you to cover any distance at all—bobbing and weaving, for example—footwork is still an integral part of these techniques. You may constantly be shifting the weight from left to right but not going anywhere. This kind of weight transfer, though, is the only way to move quickly. If you move only at the waist, you'll be too slow.

- **Move at the last possible moment and stay in close**—This isn't a macho thing, but it sure feels good when you pull it off. The idea is to slip punches or pull away just enough to clear the punch. This keeps you in striking range so you can counter, and counter quickly because you haven't wasted any motion. If you get in close, this also jams the other guy, taking away his leverage. Moving at the last second prevents your opponent from changing directions and catching you with a different punch. The perfect slip, for example, would mean feeling your opponent's hand lightly graze your ear!

- **Evasion is a better choice than blocking**—If at all possible, evade an attack without using either hand. Just get out of the way. This frees your hands to counter. During the time it takes for your arm to recover from blocking a shot, the window of opportunity may be lost. Simple evasion also means less wear and tear on the joints and muscles. There will be times when you have no time for clean evasion, and blocking will be necessary. But keeping both hands free is always the better choice.

FOOTWORK: THE FIRST LINE OF DEFENSE

Footwork should always be your first choice for evasion. On the most fundamental level, footwork is what enables you to maintain the proper distance from your opponent. If you're not within striking range, you can't get hit, right? As you move into closer range, you can use pivoting and sidestepping to place you at favorable angles for countering. Even without a bob, weave, or slip, just pivoting to your opponent's outside—for example, pivoting to the outside of a left stancer (Figures 9.1 and 9.2)—enables you to avoid blows and throw counters at the same time. The most common counters that accompany the pivot would be corkscrew hooks and shovel hooks. From the *Tao*:

> *"Footwork can and will beat any kick or punch. The more adept a fighter is at footwork, the less does he make use of his arms in avoiding kicks and blows. By means of skillful and timely sidestepping and slipping, he can get clear of almost any kick and punch, thus preserving both of his guns, as well as his balance and energy for counters."*[1]

Footwork frees up both of your hands to throw fast counters without missing a beat. Though not recommended for fighting in close quarters, as a drill, try evading punches with both hands down. Try to stay within range, bobbing, weaving, slipping, and rolling, but without parrying or blocking. You may not be well protected for infighting, but at longer ranges, notice how much easier you move when both hands aren't up all the time.

Figure 9.1
Evasive pivoting

Figure 9.2

THE SLIP

The slip is used at longer-to-medium-range distances against straight punches.[2]

The underlying principle of the slip is a counterintuitive one: you must move into the punch. This takes away your opponent's leverage. If you don't get in close enough, you run the risk of a pot shot. You'll also be too far away to get in a counter. Get in close and be sure to jam him.

To slip right from the on-guard position, push off with your left foot—just as you would when throwing a drop shift—and angle off to the right. (Figures 9.3 and 9.4) Though, not always possible, ideally, toes of both feet should be angled off at about 30° from the reference stance line. Hunch up your left shoulder and turn it towards the target, same as you would if you were throwing a rear cross. Keep both hands up, tuck in you chin, and be ready for a counter hook.

The slip is different from some of the other evasive moves, because you actually do take up real estate by moving forward. And even though you may not be throwing a punch, you still need to shift your weight forward via footwork.

Figure 9.3
Slipping right

Figure 9.4

Bruce's description of the footwork for slipping sounds a lot like the footwork for the rear cross, particularly the pivot of the left heel:

> *"The key to successful slipping often lies in a little movement of the heel. For example, if it is desired to slip a lead to the right so that it passes over your left shoulder, your left heel should be lifted and twisted outwards. Transferring your weight to your right foot and twisting your shoulders will set you up nicely to counter."*[3, 4]

Remember never let that torso overtake the right leg. Even though you are leaning forward and to the right, you should be able to look straight down and see your knee. Your feet should always be under you.

To slip left, you can angle off by stepping forward and to the left with your front foot. (Figure 9.5) Or take a long step with your left foot, which will overtake your right foot. (Figure 9.6) You actually push off with the left foot as you step in with it. This momentarily puts you in left lead stance and in prime position to throw a "haymaker" with your strong (right) side in the back. To get right back with your strong side forward, just follow up with a left cross.

Figure 9.5
Slipping left

Figure 9.6

Application

For the most part, you will want to slip to the outside. Against a right stancer, then, you'll slip to the left, his outside. Against a left stancer, you'll slip to the right. This opens up several openings for you while your opponent is turned around and can't counter:

> *"It is possible to slip either a left or right lead although more often used and safer against a right lead. The outside slip, that is, to the left of an opponent's right lead or to the right of an opponent's left lead, is the safest position, leaving the opponent unable to defend against a counterattack."*[5]

To successfully pull off a slip, you've got to have impeccable timing. Because the slip is a long-to-medium-range move, timing is determined by footwork. He may be throwing "feeler" jabs or you may be stalking each other at long range. Look for patterns he may be falling into. You may time him on his way in, before he even starts to move, or as he's retracting the hand. And you can set him up for any of the three via Attack By Drawing (ABD). In all three cases, you can use footwork and timing to move in and bridge the gap.

A successful slip is like hitting a home run. All the elements—timing, distance, and technique—have to come together. You want to slip in just about as close as you dare. If your opponent's hand grazes your ear, consider it a perfect slip.

THE WEAVE

Unlike the slip, in which you move into the punch and angle off to either side, the weave is a purely lateral move. Think windshield wiper. The main objective of the weave is to keep your head elusive.[6]

It can be used as a purely defensive move to get out of the way, but it is also helpful when you are moving in for an attack. Instead of charging in as an easy target, weave your way in so your opponent has a hard time countering you. Because it is a lateral move, the weave is employed at close range or as you're moving into close range.

Footwork for the Weave

Once again, the weave is a JKD technique for which most people underestimate the importance of footwork. What you see is only the upper body moving at the waist and the head avoiding the punch. To get your head out of the way quickly, though, requires a very subtle shift in weight.

Even though you may not take up any space at all while weaving, you are always shifting your weight from one foot to another. So if you're weaving to the left, push off from your right foot and transfer most of your weight to the left. The weight distribution after this shift should be about 60% on your left foot and 40% on your right. If you weave to the right, push off your left foot and onto your right.

This weight transfer will be imperceptible to the untrained eye, but you'll be able to tell if you're doing it correctly by watching your left heel. When you push off the left foot and onto the right, your left heel will be raised slightly higher than usual. Your left knee will also turn in a bit. When you push off your right foot, your heel will come back down and the left knee returns to normal position.

Now try rocking back and forth between weaving left and weaving right. Notice how your left heel raises to push you to the right and lowers to absorb the weight transfer as you push to the left. This is a prime example of how important body feel is, because you can't really see that weight transfer. You're going to have to feel it. Make sure you can feel all the potential energy chambered on the medial sides of your legs and in the balls of your feet. Know that you could shift left or right at any time.

A variation of this footwork would actually involve a push-off in which your feet actually leave the ground. You can use this if you have to take up extra real estate to clear a punch. It would look something like a fast sidestep or a sidestep push-off. This step can be used not only to weave but also to throw a hook as you weave. If you are weaving left, you can throw a right hook because the punch is traveling in the same direction as you are. If you weave right, you can simultaneously throw a left hook. (Figures 9.7–9.8) You can generate quite a bit of power this way, because, one, you've got all your body weight behind it. And, two, if you've weaved right, for example, your body has extra distance to travel left. That extra distance gives you more momentum—and power—as you weave left. Hooking out of this side-to-side movement keeps your opponent guessing. You are not only elusive, but he also has no idea whether or not you're going to throw a punch as you're avoiding him.

Figure 9.7

Figure 9.8

Upper Body Mechanics of the Weave

While footwork is essential for successful weaving, as with all evasive moves, the weave starts with the head. Because the objective is to get our noggins out of harm's way, the noggin moves first. And as with all movement in JKD, the head does not move independently of the torso, so the first motion of weaving is actually at the waist.

When you weave left, you bend slightly at the waist to your left. (Figure 9.11) Notice how my head and torso are directly over my left knee. As you weave right, bend slightly to the right. (Figure 9.10) It's important to move enough to your left or right so that you clear punches, but it's also important that you don't move so much, you're off balance. Again, notice how my head and torso are directly over my right knee.

Over-weaving is the most common problem I see. Stay within that base of support. To check your technique, weave right and look straight down. If you are looking at a point to the right of it, then your torso has overtaken your feet, and you are off balance. If you're looking right over your knee or to the inside of it, you are within the boundaries set by your foot position and are balanced. Your footwork should put you in a position that allows you to clear an attack and remain balanced.

Finally, because the weave is a way of maneuvering at close range, keep those hands up—more so than you would in your regular long-range stance.

Figure 9.9

Figure 9.10

Figure 9.11

Examples of balanced weaving—*To weave right, I step out at a 30–45° angle. My head is directly in line with my right knee. Though much of my weight has shifted to the right, I am well balanced. As I weave left, notice my head is directly over my left foot. Again, my center of gravity is within the base of support determined by the position of my feet, and I am well balanced.*

Figure 9.12

Figure 9.13

Over-weaving—*Notice how my head and torso, in both cases, overtake my feet. This means my center of gravity is outside the base of support. It wouldn't take much to knock me off balance.*

Notes on Application

Remember you only need to weave when you are within striking distance or as you are advancing into that range. Otherwise, it's just wasted motion. You do not weave just for the sake of weaving. Also always remember to look for an opening as you're weaving. Take advantage of the extra power it affords and the confusion it creates.

As we'll soon discuss, you'll most likely combine the weave with the bob. When you do, if you bob and weave with balance and control, you'll always be in position to throw a hook, cross, uppercut, or corkscrew out of a bob or weave. This makes you extremely shifty and dangerous in close quarters. Against taller opponents, it helps you work your way inside to jam them, taking away their punching leverage.

If you do use the side step/weave with a punch, remember, as with the straight lead, you'll want to make contact with the target before your foot hits the ground. In this way, you take full advantage of the weave by putting your body into the punch.

DUCKING

While it leaves fewer countering options, ducking is probably one of the safest evasive moves. It's purely vertical. Unlike the weave, you won't get caught on the wrong side of a punch. Regardless of whether the punch is coming from the left hand or right, if you duck straight under it, you're safe. You also don't have to worry about whether it's a straight punch or a hook. It's not as efficient at avoiding straight punches as the slip, but if the attack is coming fast and furious you may not have the luxury of discerning between a hook and a straight. And it doesn't matter which side the hook is coming from. Whatever it is, you just move under it and you're safe. Just be sure to watch out for uppercuts. [7, 8]

How to Duck

Believe it or not, despite its expediency, the duck should require very little effort. Think of it as a collapsing of the body. Quickly tuck your knees up and let gravity take you down. At the same time, bend forward at the waist. You should look like an accordion as it collapses on itself. (Figure 9.14) The lack of effort and the effect of gravity are what make this the go-to technique when you need to get out of the way fast.

Application

Because you are only changing your height when you duck, you may have fewer countering options than you do with the bob and weave, in which you change both height and angle. Still, if you're in close, you might find openings for throwing tight hooks or an uppercut with either hand on the way up.

Figure 9.14
Ducking

THE BOB AND WEAVE

The weave is usually used with the bob. The bob gives you the added elusiveness of changing your height, while the weave changes your angle. Changing both at the same time can make you very hard to hit. Bruce referred to the combination of the bob and weave as "body sway."[9]

Also known in boxing circles as the "V-Slip," the path of the bob and weave looks something like the letter "v" or "u." The bob and weave usually starts with a weave or when you've just come out of throwing a hook or cross (Figure 9.16). In either case, your body is shifted more towards one side than the other. This is the top of your "u." To bob under the punch, you'll need to bend at the knees.[10]

The important thing here is that you get your center of gravity low. Don't be lazy. Bend at the knees, not just the waist. As you bend your knees, start shifting your weight to the other foot (Figure 9.17). So, if you bob and weave to your left, you'll start out on the right side, bend your knees, and as you come up, shift the weight to your left foot as you would for a regular weave and finish at the top of the "u" (Figure 9.18). Again, as with an isolated weave, never let your torso overtake your knee.

Just as you would with ducking, let gravity help you when you bob. Don't think of the downward portion of the bob as a movement that requires a lot of effort. You bend the knees and let your center of gravity drop down. It should be somewhat effortless. Again, it might be helpful to think of it as a passive "collapsing" of the knees instead of an active bending of the knees.

Application

The great thing about the bob and weave is that it keeps you elusive while opening up all sorts of striking opportunities. You can bob and weave left and counter with a rear cross or rear hook at the top. Bob and weave right and come up with a right hook or corkscrew at the top. Or throw an uppercut on the way up in either direction. If you throw a straight punch (rear cross or corkscrew) do so on the way up, not down. This allows you to take advantage of vertical ground reaction force, and if you're on the way down, chances are you need to clear a punch before launching an offensive.

As for defensive considerations, you do need to be careful not to get caught on the wrong side of the "u" when a punch is coming. If the punch is coming from the left (your opponent's right)—say, a straight right or right hook, the punch is traveling from your left to your right. In this case, you'll need to bob and weave to your left to pass under the punch (Figures 9.17 and 9.18).

Likewise, if your opponent throws a rear cross or left hook, the punch is traveling from your right to your left. In this case, bob and weave to the right and v-slip under the punch (Figure 9.19 and 9.20).

When you come out of a bob and weave as Bruce noted, the hook is often the preferred option and can be extremely powerful, as we've already mentioned, when combined with a side step (Figure 9.21):

> *"The art of swaying renders the fighter more difficult to hit and gives him more power, particularly with the hook. It is useful in that it leaves the hands open for attack, improving the defense and providing opportunities to hit hard when openings occur."[11]*

Figure 9.15

Figure 9.16

Figure 9.17

Figure 9.18

Figure 9.19

Figure 9.20

Figure 9.21
V-slip followed by a hook

THE SNAP BACK

The snap back or pull back is simply a linear movement backwards and away from a straight punch, usually a jab. It is purely linear and, unlike the shoulder roll, doesn't involve any rotation.

Mechanics and Footwork for the Snap Back

As with all our other defensive maneuvers, you need to move your head out of the way first, and you accomplish this by moving your torso at the waist. As the punch comes in, bend at the waist straight back. Bend just enough to clear the punch. Just like the weave, leaning your torso in the direction you want to move has the added benefit of gravity pulling you in the same direction. Now that your body, and more important, your head, have been set into motion away from the punch, the feet can follow.

Push off from your front foot as you're picking up the back foot. It's simply a regular push step backwards, that's all. You want to keep that left heel off the ground for two reasons. One, there is no rotational component to this move that requires you to lower the heel. And, two, by keeping the heel up, you still have some spring to work with, which will enable you to counter or move in another direction.

Application

The snap back, as we've mentioned is usually used to avoid straight punches. It can be used as a form of setting up your opponent if he is in a pattern of throwing lazy jabs. You can pull back, pull back, pull back, and when the time is right, move in and time him with a straight of your own. This is a pretty nifty counter, because you have the extra power provided by the arch in your back. You've got some extra distance to travel, which gives you more momentum. The trick is to use your abs to spring you forward into action. Think of it as a really fast sit-up. Obviously, the faster you snap forward, the more power you'll have in the punch.

If, however, you are using the snap back to get out of the way of a combination attack, you really can only use it once. Do not pull back twice. For example, if your opponent throws a double jab, you don't have time to pull back twice. He's going to catch you. This is because after the first snap back, you have to move forward and back into position so you can pull back again. This all occurs along the same linear plane. Your opponent is going to throw a straight, retract, and throw another straight a lot faster than you can pull back your entire torso, move it forward return to the on-guard position, and then back again. You'll lose every time.

To remedy this, combine the snap back with another evasive move, one that takes the train off the tracks. This is usually a lateral move of some kind. Snap back away from the first straight (Figure 9.22), then angle off with a shoulder roll (Figure 9.23), weave, or slip to avoid the next straight punch.

Figure 9.22

Figure 9.23

Evading the double jab—Pull back first (Figure 9.22) and then angle off with a weave (Figure 9.23)

SHOULDER ROLL

The shoulder roll differs from the snap back by incorporating a rotational component to the evasion. You turn away from the punch, which moves you in two directions—back and to the side—as opposed to only side-to-side or only straight back. With it, you can avoid straight punches, mostly jabs, and you can also roll laterally to avoid hooks.

Figure 9.24

Figure 9.25

Figure 9.26

Angles of evasion—Pull back (Figure 9.24). The angle is 180° straight back. Lateral weave (Figure 9.25) to the left. Shoulder roll with step back at a 45° angle (Figure 9.26).

Upper Body Mechanics

Once again, you'll move the head/torso before anything else. The shoulder roll involves both a pull back and a turn at the waist either to the left or right. Most of the time, though, you will be turning to the left to avoid jabs (Figure 9.26). As you bend slightly back and turn at the waist, hunch up your shoulder and tuck your chin into it.

The idea with the shoulder roll is that you want to stay in close so you can counter. Even if your opponent throws out a punch and makes contact, he only gets your shoulder while your chin is tucked safely away. Even more important is that the roll, in Bruce's words, "nullifies the force of a blow" because you move your body in the same direction as the punch.[12]

Based on the equation for impulse, by rolling with the punch, you increase the time during which you have contact with your opponent's fist. This decreases the force of his punch. The roll, then, keeps you from bearing the brunt of an attack and turns it into a mere glancing blow.

We already talked about rolling left and back to avoid lead punches, and this is the direction you'll roll most of the time. Depending on the situation, though, you may sometimes need to roll to the right. It's less safe to do this, obviously, because you expose the centerline, but at close quarters or if the punch is coming at a particular angle from your left, you may need to roll right, usually to avoid a hook. To do this, turn at the waist to your right and hunch up your left shoulder.

Because the shoulder roll requires you to turn at the waist, your hand position will change, too. As you roll right, you'll drop your right hand from its regular on-guard position. Since you've turned to the left, if you keep your hand up, it's going to be turned all the way around with you. The only option you'll have from there is a back fist. Plus, you'll leave your whole right side unguarded. But if you drop the front hand slightly, you keep it in a better position to fire a counter. By lowering the hand, you keep it in front of you and in line with the opposition (Figures 9.26 and 9.28), so you can throw a straight lead, an uppercut, or hook, either as you're rolling or after you've completed the roll. When you do this, however, do not straighten the arm completely. Keep the elbow bent between 90 and 135 degrees, and keep the arm loose and relaxed and ready for anything.

While all of this bending, turning, rolling, and arm straightening is going on, don't neglect the left hand. Keep it by your chin at all times. You may also want to incorporate a parry with the shoulder roll. As we'll discuss in the section on parrying, this will serve as a good gauge of distance and can also be used to set up your opponent.

Figure 9.27

Figure 9.28

***Shoulder roll**—Check points for the shoulder roll: turn at the waist, hunch lead shoulder, lower the lead hand, transfer weight to back foot. Lower the back heel and raise the heel of the front foot.*

Footwork and the Shoulder Roll

Because there is some rotational movement with the shoulder roll, the footwork is very much like that of the pulling hook. You will always transfer your weight from one foot to another in the direction you are moving. So if you're rolling left, just as you did with the pulling hook, lower the left (back) heel to the ground as you raise the right heel. The toes of both feet should be pointing backwards at about 30–45° off the stance reference line. You transfer your weight from a 50/50 distribution to 60% in the back foot and 40% in the front foot.

If you are only rolling laterally, you do the same. If you're rolling left, you still transfer the weight to the left leg. The only difference is you'll bend to the left a bit more and not back (Figure 9.25). If you are avoiding a hook and roll right, transfer your weight from a 50/50 distribution to 40% in the left leg and 60% in the right leg.

In all cases, you'll find that the rotational bend at the waist is facilitated by this footwork. You cannot bend and turn nearly as quickly or with as much range of motion without adjusting your foot position.

Application

The shoulder roll against an uppercut is a classic boxing move. As Bruce wrote, this variation of the shoulder roll is "backward and away." [13]

Floyd Mayweather, Jr. is a master of this move. Because it's used at close quarters, it is extra tight. Your shoulder will be hunched up closer, and your right arm will be tucked in right at your side and bent at a 45-degree angle. A regular shoulder roll against a straight punch would have your front hand out and further away from your body so that you can throw a longer range punch. But against an uppercut, you want to make yourself as small a target as possible. You also want to keep your arms in tight both for protection and to enable you to throw an equally tight counter.

Rolling can be preferable to pulling back, because it moves you out of harm's way by moving back and/or angling off, and it keeps you in closer range and in better position to counter. Bend a little extra forward at the waist along with your footwork, and the punch should just pass over your right shoulder. Now you're really close to the target and have a better chance of landing a fast counter.

Because of the rotational nature of the shoulder roll left, the rear hand becomes an excellent choice for a counter attack. Once you've rolled, there's a whole lot of power loaded up on your left side. You're turned further left than normal, so you have extra room to uncoil into the shot. You've also got more weight in your back leg, which means you'll be throwing more weight into the punch as well.

But the rear hand isn't your only choice. When you lower the lead hand and keep it in front of you, you also have all kinds of options there, too.

PARRY

A parry is the deflection and redirecting of your opponent's attack and is not the same as a block. While the block is the least desirable defensive measure, the parry can be a very useful gauge of distance and a tool to lull your opponent into a motor-set pattern.

How to Parry

The main parry in JKD employs the rear hand and usually accompanies a shoulder roll. It is almost always used to deflect—not block—a straight punch, usually a jab. The important thing to remember about all parries is that you never want to over-parry. The motion should be firm, crisp, and short—no more than 3–4 inches—just enough to change the direction of the attack. Usually your opponent's jab should pass just over your shoulder.

As Bruce noted, you want to parry as you're stepping backwards (Figures 9.29 and 9.30). Same idea as evasion—the priority is to evade, or in this case, deflect, the attack:

> "Against a very fast fighter or one with a marked superiority of height or reach, it is often necessary to step backwards when making a parry. When parrying with a step backwards, the parry should be taken as the rear foot moves backwards in the course of breaking ground. In other words, the parry should be formed with the step back and not after it has been completed." [14]

Your left hand starts from where it is in the on-guard position—by your chin. As you step back, move your left hand from left to right just in front of your face about 4 to 6 inches, no more (Figure 9.31). Your hand should be open and firm, and you'll deflect the blow mostly with the palm of your hand. It's so important that you not parry any more than you need to. Inexperienced fighters tend to get excited when the punches come in and the adrenaline's pumping and over-parry (Figure 9.32). This creates openings for the opposition. Don't help him!

Figure 9.29
Parry as you step backwards.

Figure 9.30

Another important point about parrying that is related to this is the timing of your parry. If you parry too early, you will have to reach out to meet the punch, which again, takes you out of the on-guard position. If you reach out to the punch, your opponent is not yet fully committed to his attack and can easily change direction.[15]

Figure 9.31
Efficient, correct parry—I use my left hand just enough to change the direction of the jab. My hand is still close enough to my face to protect it.

Figure 9.32
Over-parrying—Here I've pushed the jab out of the way too much. I'm using too much effort and leaving my mug wide open.

THE CANTILEVER: A VARIATION OF THE PARRY

In Old School boxing circles, the Cantilever is another name for a low line semi-circular parry. If someone throws a drop shift, you can step back altogether and go for his head, which is probably wide open for a straight punch of some kind. Or you can parry the low line shot with your front hand and deflect it downward and counter with a rear cross. The disadvantage of this, of course, is that one of your hands is occupied, but in some cases, deflecting the blow may be more useful than stepping back.[16, 17]

A more useful situation in which to use this technique, though, is against kicks coming your way. You've seen Bruce do this a million times in the movies. From the on-guard position, his front hand simply hinges at the elbow so that his forearm is parallel to the ground. With the palm of his hand, he firmly deflects his opponent's kick slightly downward. Sometimes he just uses it to make contact so he has an idea of his opponent's kicking range. This is always accompanied by some footwork. Either a simple step back or a pendulum back, depending on how deep the kick is coming in (Figures 9.33 and 9.34).

Figure 9.33
Parrying a kick

Figure 9.34

Other Applications for the Parry

I've already referred several times to the use of the parry as a means of setting up your opponent. Here's how. If a lot of jabs are coming your way, step back, shoulder roll, and parry. Easy does it. Let him get used to the laid back pace, and let him get used to the contact of your deflection. Parry…parry…parry (Figures 9.36 and 9.37). Then choose your shot. Shoulder roll and make him miss. Don't parry this time (Figure 9.38). The lack of contact should disrupt his rhythm and may even set him slightly off balance. While he's dealing with this, snap forward and counter with a stiff rear cross (Figure 9.39)

You can do something similar with the uppercut and shoulder roll. Remember when you roll away from an uppercut, you keep your front arm in close and bent at a 90-degree angle. Meet the punch with that hand. Give him contact with his next shot. Then on the next uppercut, pull in everything tight and just roll. Make him miss. This should really leave him open and vulnerable, and given the nature of the uppercut, it should throw him quite a bit off balance if he's expecting to connect with something. While he's in this state, you can easily counter with a rear cross. The roll puts you in a position that loads up the power on your left side.

Figure 9.35

Figure 9.36

Figure 9.37

Figure 9.38

Figure 9.39
Using the parry to set up patterns

BLOCKS

I've saved the block for last, because it is the least preferable of all the defensive techniques. I use the word "defense" here and not "evasion" because with a block, well, you just stand there and take it. Of course, the block is a necessary tool. There will be times when an attack comes so fast that it's just too hard to get out of the way.

But the block is your last resort. It's slow. You block the punch and then you hit. It's a two-step process. It's much better to hit as your opponent's moving in. That way, he doesn't have time to recover.

The other thing that makes blocking least desirable is that it's hard on the body. There is a distinction between parrying and blocking. When you parry, you use your hand merely to deflect force. When you block, your arm is bearing the brunt of that force. Bruce described it in pretty graphic detail:

"Parrying is more refined than blocking, which uses force and causes contusion of the tissues, nerves and bones. Blocking should be used only when it is necessary because it weakens rather than conserves bodily force. A well-delivered blow, even if blocked, will disturb balance, prevent countering and create openings for other blows." [18]

Strategy aside, over the long haul, this is a definite advantage of JKD over other arts that emphasize blocking. Imagine the wear and tear on your body over 10, 20, 30 years. And if your facing off with a weapon like a knife or sword, forget it. Blocking isn't even an option then.

COUNTERING WITH BLOCKINGS

It may be less efficient than evasion, but blocking does open up its own opportunities for countering. Just remember that whenever your opponent throws any kind of punch or kick, there's an opening somewhere for you to counter.

If, for example, he throws a right hook and you block with your left arm (Figure 9.40), he's wide open for you to sneak in a rear cross where he's left himself wide open (Figure 9.41). You can do the same, of course, with the right hand. If he throws a left hook at you. Take it on the right arm, and then throw a lead corkscrew.

Another variation would be to throw an uppercut as a counter. If he throws a low hook from either side, block with your arms and throw an uppercut where he's open. If he throws a hook low to your right, counter with a right uppercut because that's the side where he'll be open. If he throws a low hook to your left (Figure 9.42), counter with a left uppercut (Figure 9.43). The idea is to throw a punch from the side where he's left himself open.

Figure 9.40

Figure 9.41

Figure 9.42
Countering with blocking

Figure 9.43

CHAPTER TEN

KICKING

Kicking is usually more difficult to learn than upper body techniques because: 1) we use our hands for so many things in our daily lives and 2) we have to push around a lot more weight to move our legs than we do to move our arms. Throwing around that additional weight, by the way, also requires a higher level of physical conditioning.

Still, the addition of kicking to your arsenal opens up a whole new world of options. You will be dangerous from longer ranges, and the opposition will have to worry about a set of attacks in low line. And kicks performed correctly have a lot more body weight behind them than punches. Should you land a kick, then, it is potentially much more devastating than a punch.

MECHANICS OF KICKING
While kicking may feel more foreign to us than hand techniques, the mechanical principles behind kicking are the same as they are for punching. First we'll discuss those mechanics that are common to all the kicks. Then we'll delve into the specifics of each category.

The Burst
In the same way that all punches require a variation of the push off, all kicks require a type of footwork called *the burst*. Its main function is to get your kicking leg up as quickly as possible. This is where all the hard work takes place, because your leg weighs a lot more than your arm. The higher and faster you can get that kicking leg up, the faster and more powerful your kicks will be. Perfecting the burst literally gives you a leg up on the opposition.

The burst is really a close relative of the shuffle step, but instead of shuffling backwards, you move forward to issue a kick. The principles are the same, though—replacement footwork and getting gravity to work for you. We touched on this subject in the biomechanics chapter when we explained torque and force couples. To perform the burst, you have two forces acting in opposite noncolinear directions. From the stance, you push off the ball of the left foot and pull with the toes of your right foot. You should feel like you're digging into the ground with the toes of your front foot. If you were on grass you would dig up a clump of the earth in a pulling motion not too dissimilar from the way horses hoof the ground.

That digging in with your toes gives you the leverage to pull your center of gravity. It is a downward, pulling back motion. At the same time you pull, you also push upward and forward with your left foot. These forces are applied in opposite directions, which provide the torque needed to move your front leg up.

Another nuance of the burst that will help you get that leg up is slightly offsetting your center of gravity by shifting your weight forward just as you did with the straight lead. In this case, though, lift your front foot ever so slightly—leaving just enough room to be able to slip a credit card under your heel (Figures 10.1–10.2)—no more than that. You won't be able to see it, but you should feel it. This makes you somewhat unstable, thereby minimizing the inertia to overcome.

Figure 10.1

Shifting weight to the front

Figure 10.2

With your weight slightly forward and concentrated in the toes of your front foot, dig downward into the ground and pull back as you push upward and forward with the left foot. Pull your leg up quickly. As you do so, the mass of your leg will cause your center of gravity to shift slightly back. There will be a moment when both feet are not touching the ground (Figure 10.4). Again, you are falling into position with the help of our friend gravity. At the end of the burst, your weight will have shifted from the front leg entirely to the back leg (Figure 10.5).

Figure 10.3

Figure 10.4

Figure 10.5

Shifting the center of gravity

Figure 10.6

If you've seen any Bruce Lee movies, you know that he would often fake a straight lead and then go into a kick. The tactical reason for this is to bridge the gap, but there is also a side benefit to preceding a kick with a straight right. When you throw a straight, you transfer your weight to your front foot as you extend your right hand (Figure 10.8). As we mentioned, you want your weight up front so you can dig into the ground and pull your leg up. Throwing a straight requires you to transfer more of your weight up front than you normally would from a stationary position. Retraction of the front hand further contributes to this pulling back motion, giving you extra momentum for raising the leg (Figure 10.9).

Figure 10.7

Figure 10.8

Figure 10.9

Figure 10.10

Pulling motion of lead hand*—Retracting the hand following a straight or fake requires a pulling action. This gives you extra momentum for raising your kicking leg.*

As you pull the lead leg up, the rear foot, as always, is the distance regulator. Where your back foot lands determines where your kicking foot makes contact. The back foot can land anywhere from the same place it started, to a few inches forward, to replacing the location of the lead foot, or even surpassing the original position of the front foot as is often the case with the sidekick.

The burst is a difficult move to describe or even observe. Its components are so nuanced you really need to practice and always, always, always pay attention to body feel. Use the push/pull principle and the distance covered by your back foot as your guides.

Figure 10.11 **Figure 10.12** **Figure 10.13** **Figure 10.14**

Figure 10.15 **Figure 10.16** **Figure 10.17** **Figure 10.18**

Left foot determines distance—The leg comes up in exactly the same way but between Figures 10.11–10.14 and Figures 10.15–10.18 a few inches forward or backward can determine whether or not you'll reach the target.

A Leg Up on the Competition

When performing the burst, the leg comes up in a very specific way. Raise the leg at such an angle that you can throw any kick—front, hook, or side—from the same position. This keeps you non-telegraphic and your opponent guessing.

As you come out of the burst, do not let your lower leg just dangle straight down from the knee. If you do, your only option is a straight kick. Instead, raise it up at about a 45° angle. From this angle, you can still go into a straight kick, hook, or sidekick. The movement is the same for all three. They should all look the same on the way up. Most of the differences between these three kicks, as we'll later see, are determined by what happens at the knee joint.

It's crucial that your knee is bent as it comes up. I see a lot of people cheating by taking the leg up already extended at the knee (Figure 10.20). This will only slow you down! You're also going to miss out on all of the snap that comes from extending at the knee joint. Because your foot is so far from the axis of rotation, it takes a lot more effort to raise the leg. Make sure you get that knee up as high as possible. Once you do, the rest is cake. You simply whip out from the knee. But if your leg isn't high enough, it's very difficult to generate power.

It's also telegraphic. If you're lazy and take the leg up already extended, your opponent knows for sure you aren't throwing a sidekick. He can read you and come over the top of your extended leg and beat you with a kick of his own (Figures 10.21–10.22).

Figure 10.19
Proper raising of kicking leg

Figure 10.20
Failure to take the leg up with bent knee

Figure 10.21

Figure 10.22

I telegraph my kick and allow Ted—who is using proper technique—to come over the top of my leg with a kick of his own. Don't be lazy! Never raise your kicking leg already extended.

Position of the Knee

To increase strain energy, as you raise the front leg, never let your front knee overtake your hip. This is analogous to throwing a hook punch, in which you never want your fist to overtake your hip. Keeping your knee a hair behind your front hip places strain on the tendons of your leg and hip, so that when you finally release your kick, you generate power via the rubber band effect (Figures 10.23–10.24).

This is where flexibility is so important. The more you can stretch out your leg and hip, the more tension you can place on them before you go into a kick. This also takes you through a greater range of motion, which will contribute to additional momentum and power.

Figure 10.43

Figure 10.44

Figure 10.45

Figure 10.46

Vertical hook—As I bring the leg up, I'm fully loaded with potential strain energy. I keep hip flexion to a minimum without compromising my upper body position. My ankle is in full plantar flexion, maximizing strain energy (Figure 10.44). Immediately after contact, I completely relax the leg (Figure 10.45) and begin retraction (Figure 10.46).

The Hook Kick

The hook kick is the most frequently used kick in the JKD arsenal because it deviates least from the stance. The straight kicks necessitate a very slight squaring off. The sidekick requires you to lean back more than any of the other kicks so you can extend the leg. But the hook allows you to issue a kick with the least disruption of the stance, making it the kick best used in combination with punches.

Figure 10.47

Figure 10.48

Figure 10.49

Figure 10.50

Figure 10.51

Figure 10.52

***Hook kick**—Just as I'm turning the hip over, the hip joint is fully extended (Figure 10.48). That kicking leg is fully loaded with potential energy and I'm ready to whip out at the knee (Figure 10.49). Immediately after impact, I completely relax the leg (Figure 10.50). By keeping my torso upright, all I have to do is lower my kicking leg (Figure 10.51) and find myself back in stance (Figure 10.52).*

More than with any other kick, it's imperative that you do not let the knee overtake the hip so that you don't lose all leverage. This is the exact same principle behind the hook punch, for which we never let the hand overtake the hip. Once your leg is up, turn your hip all the way over. This allows you to bring your leg around and all your body weight behind it. At the last possible moment, whip out your lower leg from the knee joint. As you turn the hip over and bring the leg around, let your momentum take you through the kick and allow your left foot to pivot counterclockwise so that your left toes are pointing backwards at a 30–45° angle. Again, this adds to your range of motion.

The impact surface for the hook kick can be the toe, shin, heel, instep, or the ball of the foot (Figure 10.53–10.56). The hook kick is best used at medium-to-longer ranges. You've got to be extra careful judging the distance so as not to jam yourself.

Figure 10.53

Figure 10.54

Figure 10.55

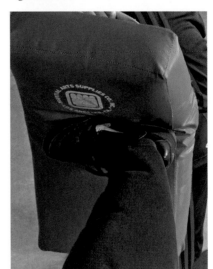
Figure 10.56

Kicking impact surfaces—Instep (Figure 10.53). Toe (Figure 10.54). Ball of foot (Figure 10.55). Flat of foot (Figure 10.56)

The Straight-Kick-Hook-Kick Continuum

Between the vertical hook kick and hook kick, lies an entire spectrum of hybrid kicks analogous to the continuum between the uppercut and hook punch. You can throw a purely vertical hook kick (Figure 10.57–10.60). And then from there is an entire range of vertical hooks with varying degrees of hooking trajectory (10.61–10.66). At the end of that spectrum is a pure hook kick (10.67–10.69). The degree of hooking depends on how much you turn the hip. If you just jerk your hip upwards without any turn, you have a purely vertical hook, or straight kick. A pure hook kick conversely requires you to turn the hip over completely. You can also change the impact surface—instep, toe, ball, heel—to create hybrid hooking and thrusting kicks.

Figure 10.57   Figure 10.58   Figure 10.59   Figure 10.60

Figure 10.61   Figure 10.62   Figure 10.63

Figure 10.64   Figure 10.65   Figure 10.66

Figure 10.67   Figure 10.68   Figure 10.69

The straight-kick-hook-kick continuum

Low Hook Kick

The low hook kick is one of the most powerful kicks in the JKD arsenal. This is due to an extreme turning over of the hip, causing a chopping down motion. It's especially useful for taking out the knee at the side of the knee joint or for hitting the nerve on the anterior thigh. The footwork for this kick contributes a lot to its power. To get around to the side of your opponent's leg, you'll need to pivot around him. Replace the location of your right foot with your left foot and pivot (Figures 10.71 and 10.72). Like the corkscrew hook, the pivoting adds torque to your kick and puts you into position. Chop down on the target with the instep of your right foot (Figure 10.73). As with any hook kick, this one flows well when preceded by or followed up with the rear cross.

Figure 10.70

Figure 10.71

Figure 10.72

Low hook kick

Figure 10.73

Side Kick

Like the straight thrust, the side kick is a thrusting kick. The difference between the two is one of positioning. You take the leg up as you would for the hook or straight kick—with the burst and at a 45° angle at the knee. From here, you turn the hip over completely as you thrust out your leg, extending it fully. This requires you to lean back at the waist more so than any other punch.

The key, though, is not to lean straight back. You actually lean at an angle. As with the hook kick, the toes of your back foot should point backwards at a 45° angle. Instead of leaning straight back, you should be leaning right over those toes with your torso pointed at the same angle as your foot. At the end of a sidekick, if you were to look down, you should be staring straight down at your toes (Figure 10.77).

Figure 10.74

Figure 10.75

Figure 10.76

Figure 10.77

Figure 10.78

Figure 10.79

Figure 10.80

Side kick—*Because it's a long-range kick, the left foot comes in past the original position of the front foot (Figure 10.75). My back foot pivots at a 45° angle (Figure 10.76) as I start to extend the leg. My upper body leans back but not straight back. I bend at the waist so that my upper body is at the same angle as the back foot. If I were to look straight down, I would be looking directly over my back foot. This allows for more stability, more power, and better recovery (Figure 10.78–10.80)*

The positioning of your upper body is crucial to the side kick, because, one, you don't want all your body weight rolling out the back. The second reason has to do with balance. When you kick, your base of support is reduced to your left foot. This is the only contact you have with the ground. To maintain balance, then, it makes sense to lean in such a way that your torso is directly over that foot. Obviously, your kicks will be much better if you are throwing them from a stable and balanced position.

Because it's our longest-reaching weapon, the side kick can be combined with a small motion of the foot that is more like a feint than a step. This is a form of PIA that can help you work your way in. Because it takes you so far away from the stance, though, the side kick must be used judiciously. It's not conducive to combinations, so if you choose to use the side kick, it better be a finisher.

Low Side Kick

The low side kick is used to do damage to your opponent's front leg. The technique for raising the leg is the same as for our other kicks. The difference is that once the leg is up, the sidekick thrusts downward and outward, so you will come down on or above your opponent's knee (Figure 10.81–10.82). A lot of JKD practitioners overemphasize the use of the low side kick as a leg obstruction technique. Really, it's only effective against a mediocre kicker who comes up with the leg already extended. If he's got a half decent kick, he's going to bring that knee up, fast and bent at an angle so that it will be very hard to stop him on the way up because his leg will be in close. It will also be hard to tell what kind of kick he's going to issue. As you try to leg-obstruct him, he might just come up over the top at the last minute and wipe you out.

If you're going to intercept or stop-hit your opponent with a kick, it's much safer to go for the solar plexus or the ribs. The torso consists of a lot more surface area than the leg, so you're less likely to miss if you go for the upper body.

Figure 10.81

Figure 10.82

Low side kick—Unlike a leg obstruction, you load up the kicking leg as you would a sidekick and come down hard on the target. It is not a mere obstruction or block.

Spinning Back Kick

The spinning back kick, though a risky venture, can be a great, unexpected attack. To execute from the stance, pick up your front foot and pivot almost a full 180°. When you finish the spin your toes should be facing straight back, opposite to the target. As you initiate the pivot, tuck your left leg in close to your body so you'll spin faster (Figure 10.84). When you plant your right foot down at 180° (Figure 10.85), let the momentum of your spinning body continue your pivot even though the ball of your foot will remain on the ground (Figure 10.86). Do not extend the leg until the last possible moment (Figure 10.87). While pivoting/spinning, raise your left leg. Keep your body upright to maintain balance (Figure 10.85). Then as you come out of the spin, thrust out your left leg and lean slightly forward as you would for a side kick (Figure 10.89). Ideally, you'll want to land the target while still spinning to take advantage of the additional torque. Unlike other martial arts, though, the spinning back kick in JKD is less of an arcing sweep kick, and more of a thrusting, side kick.

Figure 10.83

Figure 10.84
Spinning back kick footwork

Figure 10.85

Figure 10.86

Figure 10.87

The danger of this technique, of course, is that there is a moment during which your back is completely turned toward your opponent, so timing, distance, and spinning speed are crucial. To minimize the time your eyes are off the target, just before you initiate the spin, focus on the target in front of you. Then immediately turn your head so you are looking over your left shoulder and visually zero in on the target again.

The spinning back kick is good against a rusher. He bridges the gap, not you. It's more difficult for him to reach you because you're spinning in place, so you are less accessible to his front hand and foot.

Figure 10.88

Figure 10.89

Figure 10.90
Spinning back kick

Figure 10.91

CHAPTER ELEVEN

ADVANCED FOOTWORK

Most martial arts instructors have a cursory understanding of basic footwork, but this, unfortunately, is where their instruction ends. The exception to this would be fencing schools. It's no coincidence, then, that JKD, with its strong roots in fencing, would stress the importance of footwork in tactics. In most cases, though, the finer points of footwork just aren't taught, and that's in boxing gyms and dojos, too, not just in the JKD world. There seems to be a myth that when it comes to footwork, either you've got it, or you don't.

Footwork is woefully taken for granted. The small details that separate mediocre from great technique are extremely subtle and virtually imperceptible to the untrained eye. Instead of diving in and unlocking the secrets of those details, many arts and instructors just gloss over the basics often because this is where their understanding ends. If an instructor's technique is good, then he may be one of the lucky few, able to perform well naturally, but perhaps not able to convey how he does what he does. You know the old saying, those who can't do teach. Often the opposite is true, too. Those who do can't teach. This is too bad, because footwork can be taught but only by an instructor who's done his homework.[1] This is where we are so lucky to have Ted Wong's level of analysis, which rivals that of elite-level instructors of any discipline. Now, if you're one of the lucky few who's "got it," this isn't terribly exciting or useful. But for most of us who comprise the other 99.9% of the population, it's invaluable.

Sifu Wong has broken down the finer details of footwork and how they relate to tactics and force production. But perhaps even more important, he is able to convey and demonstrate those details. I see a lot of instructors talk, talk, talk, but never roll up their sleeves and get in the mud and *show* us their abilities. Whether or not you, as a student, are able to actually perform the movements is another matter, but you stand a lot better chance of *doing* once you understand how it all works. Once you can break down some of these complex moves into their separate components, you're on your way.

Finally, it's pretty difficult to learn footwork from a book. Read the explanations below and then watch the footwork in boxing, fencing, and UFC matches, and, most essentially, Bruce Lee's films. You'll start to understand how the components of tactics, speed, and force production fit together all through the magic of footwork.

THE HALF-BEAT: REAL-WORLD FOOTWORK AND BROKEN RHYTHM

The problem with most explanations of JKD footwork is that they only present the most basic steps, what we call whole-beat footwork. If you've ever studied music, you know that we count off like so: "one-and-two-and-three-and-four." "One-and" is one whole beat. This is analogous to most martial arts footwork. You step with the front foot. "One." Then land with the back foot. "And." Only after the "and" are you able to do something. You must complete the beat before punching, kicking, or changing direction.

The problem with this is that it's very, very slow. And predictable. Most arts require you to complete the whole step. "One"-"and." Hit on "two." They require you to have both feet on the ground before you can fire. In the real world, though, this can be pretty cumbersome.

Imagine what would happen if you could hit on the "and"—the half beat—not just the whole beat! You could beat (no pun intended) your opponent to the punch every time. You could fire a shot off no matter where your weight is distributed—front foot in the air, back foot in the air, with your weight mostly in your front foot or with your front foot just barely touching down. Being able to hit on the half beat exponentially increases your windows of opportunity. You can also set your opponent up by establishing a predictable whole-beat pattern and then breaking the pattern— hence, the term broken rhythm.

I call this real-world footwork, because in a real fight, we don't move exclusively in whole beats. Those who do, usually end up picking themselves off the floor. This is why Bruce was so heavily influenced by boxing and fencing. Even though most boxers aren't formally trained in broken rhythm, that's what you get. Their footwork is so much more alive than it is in other arts. Fencing strategy is actually based on half-beats. Indeed, Bruce took this notion of the half-beat from fencing authors like Aldo Nadi[2] and Julio Martinez Castello.[3, 4]

The basic footwork that we covered in the last chapter—sidestepping, pivoting, advancing or retreating, shuffle or step and slide—that's only a *fraction* of what footwork's all about. Yet, sadly, that is usually all that's taught. Half-beat footwork is what allows you to transition between those steps. It's the glue that holds everything together, allowing you to punch while you're in motion, wherever your weight is distributed, and from all angles.

TYPES OF HALF-BEAT FOOTWORK

Basic Half-Beat

This is the most basic form of changing direction on the half-beat. Say you are retreating with the step and slide. Back foot steps back and lands. "One." Front foot steps back and lands. "And." Back foot steps and lands again. "Two." Now, instead of letting your front foot land, push off with your back foot so that you are moving forward. You've just changed direction on the half beat—the "and" of "two." This is a great way to set up patterns and break them. Retreat, retreat, retreat, and then push off into an offensive with a drop-shift or a straight lead. It's also a great step to use when you pull back to evade a punch. Pull back, and before your front foot lands, push off into a counter cross or straight.

You can do the same when advancing. Step forward and the front foot lands. That's "one." Back foot slides up and lands. "And." Step forward again with the front foot. That's "two." Before your back foot lands, push off your front foot backwards. This is a change of direction on the "and" of "two." This is a great way to avoid counters that are thrown as you're advancing. You might jab and advance. Jab and advance. When your opponent counters with a jab of his own, you push back, land on your back foot, and before the front foot can land, push off that back foot and throw another jab.

The basic half-beat can also be applied to sidestepping. It's absolutely necessary to use this in close quarters. When you weave left, for instance, you might combine that with a side step to the left. Push off your right foot. The left foot lands. "One." Before your right foot lands, push to your right and weave right. "And." If you're in really close or are working your way in, you'll want to use this half-beat side step when weaving—if you don't, you're going to get caught. Imagine how slow you'd be if you were to weave left and had to wait until your right foot lands before weaving back to the right.

This half-beat side step, by the way, is great for combining with a hook. Sidestep left and hook with your right. Sidestep right and hook with your left. Weave, weave, weave, and when the window of opportunity opens, hook with either hand depending on which foot you're able to push off with.

Figure 11.1   Figure 11.2   Figure 11.3   Figure 11.4

Figure 11.5   Figure 11.6   Figure 11.7

Basic half-beat—From the starting position (Figure 11.1) I push off backwards with the front foot (Figure 11.2). Before my front foot can land (Figure 11.3) I push off forward with the back foot (Figure 11.4). This is reversing direction on the "and" or half-beat. As always when advancing, land with the heel of the front foot (Figure 11.5) and be sure to bring the back foot up the same distance (Figure 11.6) so that you end up right back in stance (Figure 11.7).

Split Step

This is a technique that Ted has referred to in seminars as the "fancy step." It may very well be my favorite step because it's fast and effortless. This step, in a nutshell, is initially stepping in one direction and falling in the opposite direction.

Linearly, it can be used for changing direction quickly forward or backward, left or right. You can use this step either while already in motion or from a stationary position. Say you step and slide forward. Step and slide. Step and slide. Then your opponent fires a jab. Lean back slightly and turn at the waist. At the same time quickly open up your stance, kind of like you would if you were doing a jumping jack. (Figure 11.9) You've momentarily got both feet in the air or barely touching the ground, and you're leaning backwards. This lets you take advantage of gravity. You're actually *falling* backwards. Land first with the front foot and before your back foot can land, push off backwards with your front foot. (Figures 11.9 and 11.10) This is the fastest and easiest way to change direction because you let gravity do most of the work. Be sure to maintain the integrity of the stance upon recovery. (Figure 11.13)

Figure 11.8   Figure 11.9   Figure 11.10

Figure 11.11   Figure 11.12   Figure 11.13

Reverse split step

Now say you're step and sliding backwards and all of a sudden you see an opening. To move forward, lean slightly forward at the waist to set your body weight in motion. At the same time, do your pseudo jumping jack. Let your back foot land first, and before the front foot lands, push forward with the back foot as you throw your punch.

The split step is great for lateral movement as well. While it's not taught formally in boxing gyms, I've seen many boxers use it to reverse direction laterally, Oscar De La Hoya being a great modern example. Ted originally noticed this step watching Carlos Ortiz in the 1960's. And you'll see quite a few examples of this in Bruce Lee's *Game of Death* footage.

To move left with the split step, lean slightly to your left. This time the step is more of a sideways jumping jack with your feet barely touching the ground (Figure 11.15). Before your left foot lands push off your right towards your left (Figure 11.16). Land with the heel of your left foot (Figure 11.17) and then bring the right foot down, again, landing first with the heel (Figure 11.19). When you've completed the step, you should be right back in your original stance (Figure 11.20).

Figure 11.14

Figure 11.15

Figure 11.16

Figure 11.17

Figure 11.18

Split step left

Figure 11.19

Figure 11.20

To split step right, lean slightly to your right (Figure 11.22), open up the stance, and allow your left foot to land first (Figure 11.23). Push off the left foot towards your right (Figure 11.24). The left foot follows and puts you right back in the stance (Figures 11.26 and 11.27).

Figure 11.21

Figure 11.22

Figure 11.23

Figure 11.24

Figure 11.25
Split step right

Figure 11.26

Figure 11.27

One thing to watch for with the split step is that you don't want to split too far. 3 or 4 inches, that's it. This is especially true of the foot that you're pushing off from. If your aim is to move to the right, don't open up so much that your left foot moves too far to the left. You'll have that much more distance to regain. Your leg will be too extended so you won't have anywhere left to spring from.

Touch Down

I referred to this step under the "weight up front" heading in *The Straight Lead*. It's used mainly with the step and slide which is a lot like walking. When your right foot is stepping, it's in the air, and much of your weight is shifted to the left (back) foot. When you step down with the right foot, you slide up with the left foot by picking it up off the ground, and much of your weight is then shifted to your front foot.

The touch down step is used should a striking opportunity present itself when your right foot is just about to touch down and most of your weight is in the back foot. Let your right heel barely touch down, but do not wait for the rest of your foot to make contact with the floor (Figure 11.29). It'll be too late! Instead, just as your right heel touches down, push off that left foot (Figure 11.30). Note that you don't wait for the back foot to advance as you would with the step and slide. Instead, your right foot barely touches the ground, and as soon as it does, pick it up (Figure 11.30) and push off from wherever your back foot is at the time (Figure 11.31).

That's half-beat, Baby! In music terms, you might say it's playing ahead of the beat, because you don't even wait for that first count to complete itself—your right foot only partially touches the ground, so you haven't fully counted "one" before you've moved forward on the "and."

The touch down not only breaks the rhythm of a fight, but it also gives you extra momentum going into the punch, because you do not plant all your weight into the ground, so there's no start-and-stop business. It requires a certain rhythm and is easily one of the more difficult steps in our repertoire, but it sure opens up a lot of opportunities.

Figure 11.28   Figure 11.29   Figure 11.30

Figure 11.31   Figure 11.32   Figure 11.33

The touchdown gives you extra momentum going into a punch

Stealing Step

The stealing step is like a changeup pitch. But instead of taking the pace down a notch, you're going to step up the speed and cadence. The stealing step gives you that little extra something that allows you to bridge the gap and/or come in deeper with your punch, which is almost always a straight lead because we're talking about a long-range shot.

With both feet on the ground, you'll slide your left (back) foot up lickety-split 3 or 4 inches (Figure 11.35). This gives you a little extra leverage for your push off. A soon as that left foot comes up, push off into your punch. I can't overemphasize the quickness of this move. It's got to be hair-trigger fast. Like a twitch—and then you explode into the punch.

Because it is a twitch, though, you don't want to use this from a stationary position. You give too much away. But if you are in a step and slide pattern it's a great way to surprise your opponent. It's also good for closing the distance on a runner and for kicking at medium ranges.

Figure 11.34
Stealing step

Figure 11.35

Stutter Step

The stutter step is like a footwork feint. Its aim is to disrupt your opponent. In the *Tao's* section on feints, Bruce wrote the following:

> *"A slight wave of the hand, a stamp of the foot, a sudden shout, etc., can produce sensory irradiations sufficient to reduce coordination. This mechanism is at the reflex level of human behavior and even many years of athletic experience cannot erase the distracting effects of extraneous stimuli."*[5]

The stutter step, then, is literally a "stamp of the foot." Like the stealing step, there is a particular staccato rhythm to it. You stamp the ground quickly with the ball and toes of your front foot. Your right foot hits the ground and then almost bounces off the floor. While your right foot is midair, push off with your left foot into an attack.

Like the stealing step, this is a twitch that can telegraph your punch, so it should be used sparingly only when you are chasing your opponent or are already in motion in a step and slide pattern. The stutter gives you a little extra momentum, and the twitch is something that should cause your opponent to react in some way that disrupts his plans and rhythm.

A variation of this is a double stutter. Stutter twice and then attack. This step is great for kicking and is more extreme than the stealing step in terms of bridging the gap.

Bouncing

The bounce is like the oil in your car. It just makes everything run smoothly. Without it, you wouldn't be able to link all the different steps and directions together without it being slow and awkward.

When you're off balance or you're heading too fast in the wrong direction and need to put on the brakes, the bounce is like a great shock absorber. Say you're making a quick retreat. Once you're out of harm's way, bounce a little on your back leg to absorb your momentum.

If you're operating from a bounce, it's going to be a lot easier to shift directions, too. Again, gravity and momentum are our friends. When you bounce, you have less contact with the ground, so it's easier to move. It's a lot easier to run uphill than it is to walk uphill. When you walk, your legs have to go through a fuller range of motion because of the longer time your foot is on the ground. When you run, you're almost bouncing. You're in minimal contact with the ground, have more momentum, and use less energy.

So if you're working off a bounce, you're able to switch into high gear much easier. You should be able to hit off a bounce, change directions off a bounce, and evade off a bounce. This is why you always hear George Foreman talking about how important it is for fighters to have bounce in their step.

Keep in mind, though, this isn't just indiscriminately jumping around.[6] If your opponent isn't in striking range, you're not going to need to bounce. That's just a waste of energy. Save it for when you need it. When you're in closer range and on high alert—that's when you need to be shifty.

Skip Step

Identified and named by George Shido, a fellow student of Ted's, the skip step is just as it sounds—a skip. You can think of it as the opposite of the touch down. In this case, all of your weight is in the front foot, and the back foot has not landed yet or has barely touched down when you skip with the front foot into another punch. The skip step is usually used as you're coming out of an attack. Say you throw a rear cross. You transfer your weight from the back to the front leg and as your back leg touches the ground, do not let your weight settle onto the back foot. Instead, go right into throwing another cross or hook by skipping into it with the front foot.

The skip step is a dangerous option mainly because you have virtually all of your weight in your front foot as you launch another offensive. This makes you very vulnerable to counters. The advantages, though, are time and momentum. The skip step can be faster for throwing that second shot because your momentum is already going forward. You also expend less energy. You'll just have to be very careful that you don't get timed on the way in.

The skip step is actually a bit safer when used with a straight thrust kick. Say your opponent comes in with a kick. Get your front leg up pronto to avoid or intercept the attack. With your leg still up skip in with your left leg for a counter straight thrust. In this way it's very similar to the touch down step. You pick up the front leg and then launch an offensive from wherever the back leg is at the time.

While the skip step can be a risky venture, it does allow you to seize the opportunity should you find all of your weight on one foot.

Figure 11.36

Figure 11.37

Figure 11.38

Figure 11.39

Figure 11.40

Figure 11.41

Figure 11.42

Skip step—*From the starting position (Figure 11.36) I lift my kicking leg (Figure 11.37). My weight is already shifted forward. From there I push off, but my back foot has not moved from its initial position when I start to push off (Figure 11.38). From the original starting point, I actually skip into the kick and am airborne by a few inches (Figure 11.39). I start to touch down at the same time as impact (Figure 11.40), but my weight has not completely settled into my left foot yet. In line with the principles of projectile motion, the skip step takes advantage of gravity to give the technique extra juice. At impact, I am just touching down with my toes (Figure 11.40) but upon completion, my leg is much more bent and I've come to rest on the ball of my foot to absorb my landing (Figure 11.41). By keeping my body upright, I'm in position for a quick recovery. All I have to do is set my front foot down and I'm back in the stance. I'm also perfectly setup to follow up with a straight lead or cross (Figure 11.42).*

Hitting on the Retreat

To bridge the gap, either you take the fight to the opposition, or he brings it to you. We've covered the former. Now let's talk about hitting while moving backwards. The primary concern is that you don't jam yourself by being too close to the target. This should be a falling step. You move backwards by pushing off the front foot (Figure 11.44), but to get your weight into the punch, keep your upper body leaning forward, so that you are pushing back and falling forward at the same time (Figure 11.45). Be sure to judge the distance carefully. You don't want to shuffle back so far from the target that you end up losing leverage. Retract the hand as you would any other straight punch (Figures 11.46 and 11.47) Hitting in reverse is a pretty effortless endeavor. Don't forget you've got your opponent's own momentum working in your favor.

Figure 11.43

Figure 11.44

Figure 11.45

Figure 11.46

Figure 11.47
Hitting while moving in reverse

Step-In/Step-Out

This is a more tactical aspect of footwork, but it's worth mentioning here before we move into application of techniques. The step-in/step-out is defined as a kind of feint in the *Tao*.[7] Because all punches and kicks involve some kind of footwork, often advancing—a step in should put your opponent on alert. You can use this tactic as a way to set up a pattern, too. Step in, step out, in, out. La la la la la la… Put him to sleep and then ATTACK!

On a subtler level, the step-in/step-out determines what tools you can use and what targets are available. After all, whenever you step in or step out, you are playing with distance.

PUTTING IT ALL TOGETHER

Of course, in JKD, we don't have forms or set patterns of any kind, but we do have drills. The purpose of these drills is not to memorize their sequence, but to acquire a certain level of control over your technique. You are striving for mobility in any direction—offensive or evasive—out of any situation, regardless of where your weight is distributed.

Here are just a few combinations to get you started. Notice how half-beat footwork links the very basic footwork together and breathes life into it. Once you've mastered these, you can start coming up with your own combinations. The possibilities are endless. Eventually, you'll be able to move exactly as you want to at will without thinking about it. The following drills are to help you develop the tools necessary to move instinctively when under pressure.

- shuffle back/push back
- push back/shuffle back (note: as soon as the back foot lands, shuffle back)
- pivot/shuffle back (note: if you pivot left, you really need to shuffle back because you are more vulnerable moving to your opponent's inside)
- shuffle back/pivot
- push back/push back/half-beat push off forward
- shuffle back/counter with kick
- shuffle back/push step forward and punch
- push back/bounce on rear foot/shuffle back
- shuffle back/stop-hit (note: if your leg is up for a kick but the other guy isn't there, follow up with a straight since your momentum is going forward already)
- bounce/split step
- bounce/bounce into a split step
- bounce/split step/shuffle back
- bounce/bounce/bounce/split step
- bounce into a pivot/split step
- slip in/pivot/shuffle back to opponent's outside (note: handy for getting out of close quarters)

Step-In/Step-Out Combos for Broken Rhythm

- step in/pause/punch
- step in/stutter step and punch
- step in/step out/half-beat forward and punch
- step in/step out/touch down and punch
- step in/step out/burst and kick
- stutter step/stutter step/stealing step and punch

CHAPTER TWELVE

SPEED

Everyone knows that Bruce Lee was lightning fast. But while he may have been born with a certain number of fast-twitch muscle fibers, he knew speed was something that could be improved with training. Some misguided souls say you shouldn't bother training like Bruce Lee because you weren't born with the same physique. True, we may never be as fast as Bruce was, but speed is a lot more complicated than that. Genetics are not the only factor. Nor is sheer speed. In fact, training more like Bruce did can only improve your speed. Indeed, as the National Academy of Sports Medicine states, "Speed is a biomotor ability that can be learned and trained by following an integrated training program."

TYPES OF SPEED

Bruce referred to 5 categories of speed in his notes. They are as follows:

1. Perceptual speed
2. Mental speed
3. Initiation speed
4. Performance speed
5. Alteration speed

Let's take a look at each in greater detail.

Perceptual Speed

Perceptual speed is just as it sounds—it's how fast you can perceive striking opportunities. In kinesiology books, this is also referred to as quickness or reaction time. This is the speed at which you react to any kind of sensory information—visual, auditory, or kinesthetic.[1]

There are a lot of traditional martial arts drills for developing this. For instance, you can have someone throw punches at a focus mitt. The mitt holder should peripherally look for the slightest possible shoulder movement, a twitch, change in facial expression—anything that might give away that a punch is about to be thrown. When the mitt holder senses this, he should try to lower the pad and make his partner miss.

There are endless variations of these types of drills. The objective of all of them is to train you to pick up on the slightest movement that will give away an impending offensive. If you're extremely sensitive to seeing these things, you'll also be able to differentiate between a fake or feint and the real thing.

A hint to better perceptual speed is to take your opponent in as a whole. Do not focus on any one particular point as you face your opponent. Bruce called this "diffusing the attention over a wider area."[2] This way you can pick up on the slightest movement from the upper or lower body, from the left or right. Plus, you won't go cross-eyed staring too intently at any one point.

Mental Speed

Bruce defined this as the speed at which you can make split decisions—what technique to use and when, how to react to your opponent's attacks, which counter to use, etc. In our kinesiology textbooks, this would also fall under the category of reaction time. In this case, though, it has more to do with decision-making than it does mere perception.

Now that you've sensed your opponent's intent, mental speed is the rate at which you can decide what to do.

The irony of this, of course, is that, ideally, you want mental speed to be *unconscious* mental speed. Your choice of weapons at the opportune time should be without conscious thought. As Bruce said in *Enter the Dragon*: "I do not hit. It hits all by itself!"

This kind of mental speed certainly has a neuromuscular component to it. In a fight you don't have time to ask yourself, "Hmm, what would work best here? An uppercut or a hook?" This is where your hours of drilling on the focus mitts pay off. While we do not have set patterns in JKD, we do know that certain combinations tend to flow better than others. If we practice these, our body remembers them and can better use them when the heat is on. Of course, sparring will help you recognize certain situations and what choices to make. The more you are exposed to such situations, the faster you'll be.

In most endeavors, from music to sports, this is a state to which we all aspire—unconscious consciousness. The joy in any art is the progression to this state. In the *Tao*, it is referred to as "*reflex control*" and is defined as a shift "from small details (mechanical performance) to larger ones, and finally to the whole action, without a thought given to any single part."[3]

Initiation Speed

Quite simply, this is how fast you can initiate a movement, whether it's offensive or evasive. This is where good form proves crucial, as Bruce defined initiation speed as the "economical starting from the right posture and with the correct mental attitude."[4] Initiation speed is overcoming inertia. This is why correct form in your stance is vitally important. If your left knee is pointed inwards, if you slightly offset your center of gravity, you have far less inertia to overcome. Your initiation speed increases exponentially. Slight changes in form and posture also increase your speed by allowing you to take advantage of gravity, as when you lean slightly to the right if you are sidestepping to the right.

Performance Speed

Defined by Bruce as "quickness of movement in carrying the chosen move into effect," performance speed is all about form and neuromuscular programming. Performance speed means cutting away any extraneous movement. Small changes may only mean a difference of milliseconds, but cumulatively, if all your techniques are as streamlined as possible, it will make a huge difference in your speed.

Whether it's performing a single move or a combination, you can only improve performance speed by practicing the actual movement. If you need to kick faster, you need to practice kicking. Punch faster, practice punching. This is simply a matter of neuromuscular programming. As you practice an actual technique, your body will figure out where to best contract and relax muscles.

Remember, our muscles usually operate as force-couples. Ideally, when you throw out a jab, your triceps act as agonists and are activated while your biceps, which are antagonists, are relaxed. When you retract your fist, the roles are reversed. Your biceps become the agonists and the triceps the antagonists. If both agonists and antagonists are activated at the same time, the result is a braking effect.[5] This will slow you down and tire you out!

The only way to perfect the complex sequence of tension and relaxation between agonists and antagonists is to practice, practice, practice in good form always. Practice as slowly as you need to in order to maintain form. Gradually increase your speed only when you have perfected the form at slower speeds. If you don't, you'll be programming your neuromuscular system incorrectly, and this can take a long time to reverse. In fact, research in kinesiology suggests that skills cannot be learned to any degree of competency unless a particular learning progression is adhered to. In other words, you cannot skip steps.[6]

Figure 13.1

Figure 13.2

Figure 13.3

Figure 13.4

Figure 13.5

Figure 13.6

Figure 13.7

Figure 13.8

2. **Lead punch/lead kick**. Another one-two combo. This time use the momentum of your retracting hand to pull your front leg up into the kick (Figure 13.10–13.11). My center of gravity shifts from front to back allowing me to raise the leg quickly.

Figure 13.9

Figure 13.10

Figure 13.11

Figure 13.12

Figure 13.13

Figure 13.14

3. **Lead kick/lead punch/cross/hook.** Follow-up the one-two with a cross and hook. Once again, during the kick I keep my upper body as upright as possible so I can move into the punch quickly (Figures 13.17–13.18). You really need to fire your abs to follow a kick with a punch. After landing the straight, I immediately retract the hand—straight out, straight in—and follow up with the cross (Figures 13.23–13.24). As soon as I've finished the cross, as I'm retracting the hand, I'm already looking to throw the hook (Figure 13.25). I'm in an open stance following the cross. The footwork for the hook puts me right back into a safer position (Figure 13.28).

Figure 13.15

Figure 13.16

Figure 13.17

Figure 13.18

Figure 13.19

Figure 13.20

Figure 13.21

Figure 13.22

Figure 13.23

Figure 13.24

Figure 13.25

Figure 13.26

Figure 13.27

Figure 13.28

OTHER COMBOS

1. **Low kick/left cross.** You can think of a low lead kick as a sub for a right hook. The footwork for one sets up for the other as it does for all cross/hook combos. In the same way you'd follow with the straight lead, you need to fire those abs to follow up with the cross (Figures 13.33–13.34). In the case of the cross, you probably need to do so to an even greater degree, as you have to rotate the hips even more to throw the cross. Once again, land on the target before your foot hits the ground and recover so you can follow up with a hook or hook kick.

Figure 13.29

Figure 13.30

Figure 13.31

Figure 13.32

Figure 13.33

Figure 13.34

Figure 13.35

Figure 13.36

Figure 13.37

Figure 13.38

2. **Low kick/left cross/low kick.** As we mentioned earlier, the hook and hook kick can be interchangeable. Here I throw a one-two in the form of a straight kick and cross (Figures 13.40–13.43). After the cross, once again, my foot position leaves me in open stance. To close it, instead of throwing a hook, I follow-up with a hook kick (Figures 13.44–13.48). At the end of the kick, all I have to do is lower my leg and I'm right back in the stance.

Figure 13.39

Figure 13.40

Figure 13.41

Figure 13.42

Figure 13.43

Figure 13.44

Figure 13.45

Figure 13.46

Figure 13.47

Figure 13.48

3. **Left cross/low kick/left cross.** Sometimes it's good to lead off with the cross (Figures 13.50–13.51), particularly against left stancers. My feet are in position to follow up with either a right hook or hook kick (Figure 13.53). In this case it's a hook kick (Figure 13.56). And just as with a boxing cross/hook/cross combo, I follow the hook kick with another cross (Figure 13.61). The hook sets up for the cross and vice versa. And as you can see, I'm once again set up to throw a hook at then end of this combo (Figure 13.64).

Figure 13.49

Figure 13.50

Figure 13.51

Figure 13.52

Figure 13.53

Figure 13.54

Figure 13.55

Figure 13.56

Figure 13.57

Figure 13.58

Figure 13.59

Figure 13.60

Figure 13.61

Figure 13.62

Figure 13.63

Figure 13.64

4. **Cross/low hook kick/hook.** Though the cross is probably the most natural technique to flow out of a hook, sometimes, you'll be in position to throw a hook punch coming out of a hook kick. Here I throw a cross (Figure 13.66), followed by a hook kick (Figure 13.71). And just as you would when you follow a kick with a straight lead or cross, use your abs to get your weight moving forward (Figures 13.73–13.74). Be sure to land the target before your foot hits the ground (Figures 13.76–13.77). Your momentum from the hooking motion of the kick adds to your hook punch since both follow the same trajectory. And as with all kick/punch combos, your center of gravity shifts from the back to the front of your base of support, allowing you to really put your body weight into the punch.

Figure 13.65

Figure 13.66

Figure 13.67

Figure 13.68

Figure 13.69

Figure 13.70

Figure 13.71

Figure 13.72

Figure 13.73

Figure 13.74

Figure 13.75

Figure 13.76

Figure 13.77

Figure 13.78

Figure 13.79

CHAPTER FOURTEEN

TOWARDS APPLICATION

Now that we have a few hand-and-feet combinations under our belts, let's add a few other elements to our bag of tricks. These are the elements that make fighting, dare I say, fun. The components of distance, timing, punching depth, and feint and fakes are what separate what Bruce called "the intellectual fighter" from the "mechanical fighter."[1] The intelligent fighter knows the whys, hows, and whens of what he does.

DISTANCE

Distance and Choice of Tools

We've already discussed how crucial distance judgment is to the power of your punches and kicks, particularly those with a straight or thrusting trajectory. Too close, and you run the risk of jamming yourself. Too far, and you'll never reach the target.

On a more subtle level, distance also determines your choice of tools. In close quarters, though kneeing is an option, it is unlikely you'll issue a kick, because your hand will reach the target and will do so much quicker than your leg. A little further away, and you know you can throw a lead hand or kick but not a hook or cross because you won't be able to reach your opponent. Even further away, and the hand is no longer an option. And at an even greater distance, well, nothing's happening. It makes no sense to be on high alert, so save your energy.[2]

The same observations can be used in reverse to eliminate possibilities of offensives against you. You know which weapons are available to your opponent. This doesn't occur consciously, of course. With enough practice, you develop a sense of distance and will simply react accordingly.

The Fighting Measure

It's common knowledge that the "fighting measure" is a key component to JKD. This is the distance that you must maintain with your opponent so that, in order for you to hit him, either he's got to move towards you first, or you must move towards him. This is a generally safe distance that is also close enough for the possibility of a successful simple attack.

When you maintain the fighting measure, then, there are only two ways to bridge this gap. Either your opponent comes to you, or you go to your opponent. Sounds pretty simple, but this is where all the fun begins! It's also where footwork and all those advanced steps come in. From a position where the fighting measure is maintained, if your opponent takes one step forward, he is in what Ted Wong likes to call No Man's Land. Likewise, if you take one step forward, you are in No Man's Land (Figure 14.2). This means your opponent can hit you or you can hit him without advancing. You'd better be on high alert and prepared to see some action.

Almost every other martial art operates in No Man's Land, including boxing. This is a distinguishing feature of JKD. We tend to fight outside No Man's Land. This is made possible by footwork, particularly the push off and the straight lead. The straight gives you a reach advantage over a conventional boxing jab. You can reach the other guy but he can't reach you. Pretty nifty.

Bruce referred to this as his fourth principle of distance in attack, which is the "constant shifting of footwork to secure the correct measure" and the "use [of] broken rhythm to confuse the opponent's distance while controlling one's own." [3, 4] What you are trying to do here is trick your opponent into moving into what he thinks is a safe distance when in fact, it's not.

Figure 14.1

Figure 14.2

The fighting measure—*The distance at which I must take a step to reach my opponent is called the fighting measure. In Figure 14.1, then, we would say I am maintaining the fighting measure. In Figure 14.2 I have stepped into No Man's Land.*

TIMING

The variables of distance and timing are inevitably interlocked in a dance of tactics. The two are inextricable from each other. Distance is used to create opportunities for timing your opponent. Just as there are only two ways to bridge the distance, there are only three ways to time your opponent—before, during, or after any kind of motion. In the *Tao*, these are labeled as the following:

1. **Attacks on the preparation.**[5] This is before your opponent even gets started. He hasn't even twitched yet but he's thinking about it. You must anticipate and catch him in this mindset before he can move. In fencing lingo, this is called a time thrust, which is a sub-category of the stop-hit.[6] For instance, because it is often expected that an opponent will jab his way in, you can often anticipate this and stop him before he even starts to move. And to get there in time, the hand must move before any other part of your body. Hand before foot…always.

2. **Attacks on the development.** Your opponent has already initiated his attack, but you've anticipated his choice and stop him dead in his tracks. This is also known as "time" attack or the stop thrust. Note that with the stop thrust, unlike the time thrust, you must avoid getting hit first. You might slip, bob, or weave, but you've got to evade the attack in some way as you counter. You need to anticipate the final line of attack because you can't very well evade while you're attacking.

3. **Attacks on completion.** Just like it sounds, you counter when your opponent is at full extension of a punch or kick or as he's retracting his hand or foot.[7] You attack on the whole beat, not the half.

Broken Rhythm: Breaking the Motorset Mode

In *The Straight Lead*, I explained how you set up a pattern by throwing the straight lead and then surprise your opponent by breaking that pattern. As I also noted in that book, human beings have a hardwired tendency towards being lulled into a motorset, trance-like state. In his fascinating book *Performing Rites: On the Value of Popular Music*, Simon Frith writes:

> "There are images of both culture and nature here (a chair, casual conversation; heat and light), the suggestion both that music shapes itself, usefully, to bodily needs, and that individual bodies are themselves absorbed into a kind of implacable sonic flow. Virtual time here describes an experience of bodilessness, an indifference to materiality, and Mertens notes the paradox that rhythmic regularity may well have exactly the same effect in dance music: disco, he suggests, also works like a 'narcotic,' 'individuating' musical experience through repetition but leaving the listener/dancer 'floating in cosmic soup,' with no aims, no desires at all."[8]

Sounds like a great state to put your opponent in! And you can, with footwork, distance, and timing. The idea is to establish some sort of pattern. This is where what I earlier called "stalking footwork" comes in. Set up a pattern of step and sliding forward. Complete each beat. One-and. Two-and. Three-and. Four-and. Five-BAM!!! Change-up the tempo and attack on the half-beat.

You can really lull the other guy into a false sense of security by retreating in whole beats and then reversing direction by attacking on a half beat. That's broken rhythm. You can apply this in any direction, too—forward and reverse, laterally by sidestepping, or curving by pivoting. Any combination of footwork and weapon choice is possible.

In terms of distance, you can trick your opponent into coming into No-Man's land. Set him up by retreating—make him come to you. And then on a half-beat as he's moving in, launch a counter (Figures 14.3–14.6). You can also offensively sneak into No-Man's land by advancing. Step and slide, step and slide, step and slide. Then change the pace by attacking on the half-beat with a touch down or stealing step.

The idea of lulling the opposition into a "motorset" state is written in the *Tao* exactly as it originated in Julio Martinez Castello's book *The Theory and Practice of Fencing*:

> "When the rhythm is broken, speed is no longer the primary element in the success of the attack or counterattack of the man who has broken the rhythm. If the rhythm has been well established, there is a tendency to continue in the sequence of the movement. In other words, each man is "motorset" to continue the sequence. The man who can break this rhythm by a slight hesitation or an unexpected movement can now score an attack or counterattack with only moderate speed; his opponent is motorset to continue with the previous rhythm and before he can adjust himself to the change, he has been hit."[9, 10]

Figure 14.3

Figure 14.4

Figure 14.5

Figure 14.6

Motorset mode—*Ted steps forward and I retreat (Figure 14.4). Ted advances again and I retreat again (Figure 14.5). The next time he advances, having established a pattern, I break that pattern by moving into No Man's Land with a drop-shift on the half-beat.*

The Stop-Hit

The stop-hit, an integral tactic of fencing, is any counter that is initiated *during* your opponent's attack. This could be an attack on preparation or attack on development. In either case you are *stopping* his offensive, either directly or indirectly. For the former, you are stopping him as he's moving in on you with a kick or punch. You throw a counter and stop him. This is defensive offensive at its most basic. In the case of indirect stop-hits, you attack as he's feinting or transitioning from one technique to another. He's not directly attacking you at that moment, but, for example, you stop him in the midst of a progressive indirect attack.

With footwork, distance, and timing, you can simultaneously defend yourself as you launch a counter or set up a pattern and lull the opposition into a perfectly planned stop-hit.

FEINTS AND FAKES

Feints and fakes add a whole new dimension to your manipulation of time and distance. Bruce went so far as to claim that "one can say JKD is built on feints and the actions connected with them."[11]

Feinting, though, is tricky business. It's got to be convincing or you could end up in more trouble than if you hadn't feinted at all. In some ways feinting a technique is more difficult than the actual technique. If you feint in any way that is unlike a real punch or kick—a different tilt of the shoulder, an unconvincing facial expression, half-hearted speed—if your opponent is a keen observer, he's going to read right through you. The tendency when throwing a feint or fake is to move slower than the real thing. Don't do this! Think of it this way. Feint or fake with all the speed, mechanics, and *mindset* as you would the real thing. The only difference is that you fall short.

This, by the way, is the difference between a feint and a fake. The feint is a slight movement—a shoulder twitch or the initial stages of a punch. For the feint, you only move your shoulder and hips. Do not move your hand or arm. The idea is that when you come out of a feint, you can launch an attack from wherever you finish the feint.

The fake is much more of a commitment with the punch or kick thrown from half to full extension. Note that if you throw a fake at full extension, your left foot is what makes or breaks you. To throw at full extension and land just short requires fine distance regulation from the push-off. This is imperceptible to your opponent but makes all the difference (Figures 14.7–14.8).

The purpose of either the fake or feint is to create a striking opportunity. If your feint looks threatening, your opponent is going to react. This could cause him to make a defensive move, which would create an opening for you to strike, or at least throw him off balance. In either case, it buys you time. While he's reacting in a way that you probably expected, you move in for the kill.

Feints also help you bridge the gap and are integral to attacks by drawing (ABD) and progressive indirect attacks (PIA). When you feint you advance just as you would for an attack, but it's much safer than just waltzing into No-Man's Land.[12] One of Bruce's favorite examples of this is to fake with the lead hand, which draws attention to the high line, followed by a kick to the low line. Not only does this help him reach the target, the very mechanics of this combination are synergistic. He uses the momentum of the faked punch to launch the kick using push-pull mechanics. You'll find example after example of this in his films.

Figure 14.7

Figure 14.8

Fake vs. the real thing—*For the fake, at full extension I land short. I use my footwork to judge the distance at which I can fully extend but land just shy of the target (Figure 14.7). For a real straight I come in much deeper. At contact my arm is not fully extended and I have room to extend through the target (Figure 14.8). Notice how much farther my right foot advances past the reference line for the real deal than it does for the fake.*

2. When you move around, the way your opponent lines himself up will tell you what his ideal position in relation to you is. This is usually nose-to-nose. Don't give him this! Always step askew so as not to line up for him (Figures 14.12–14.14). Make him uncomfortable.

Figure 14.12

Figure 14.13

Figure 14.14

Playing with alignment—*I angle off with a pivot (Figure 14.13) in an attempt to offset Ted's alignment. He adjusts so that an imaginary line should run under his left arch to the toe of his front foot. The same line should run to my front toe and under my left arch. This puts him in a more favorable position (Figure 14.14). It's in my best interest to angle off again and disrupt his preferred alignment.*

3. Don't forget pivoting and angling off to the side. Unlike boxing, many arts don't even have these kinds of maneuvers. They require you to square off all the time. Take advantage of this! Move laterally and pivot to open up angles (Figure 14.15).

Figure 14.15

4. Whenever you attack, be ready to counter. Once you're inside, bob and weave to change height and angle. This is not only to evade counters, but to create openings as well (Figure 14.16).

Figure 14.16

5. Always occupy your centerline while moving away from your opponent's centerline. A good stance and good footwork will accomplish this.

6. Adapt. Ted Wong likes to tell a story of how Bruce once asked him what single quality is most important to a fighter. "Toughness?" Wong asked. "Speed? Technical ability? I named everything I could think of. Bruce said 'no' to all of them. 'Go home and think about it,' he said. So I went home and made an even longer list. The next day I saw him, the answer was still 'no, no, no, no, no.' The answer, he said, is 'adaptability.' I'll never forget that. Look at Ali. When he fought Foreman, no one gave him a chance. Foreman was just knocking people out left and right. Ali's plan was to use footwork, but he couldn't keep up with Foreman, so right then and there he adapted by employing the rope-a-dope. That wore Foreman out. That's adaptability." If something ain't workin' remember that the definition of insanity is doing the same thing over and over and expecting different results. Change things up. If you can't get in through the front door, sneak in through the back. You've got a lot of tools at your disposal. Use them.

One shot deal: single angle attack

CHAPTER FIFTEEN

APPLICATION: THE FIVE WAYS OF ATTACK

I f you are at all familiar with Bruce Lee's writings, then you know that the Five Ways of Attack were among the last subjects entered in his notebooks. Using the elements discussed in the previous chapters and the weapons now at our disposal, let's take a look at each of the Five Ways.

SIMPLE ANGLE ATTACK (SAA)

The simple angle attack is a one-shot deal. It's the most simple of all the attacks, and this ironically makes it the most difficult to execute. A successful simple attack depends entirely on timing, distance, and sheer speed. Because you have to bridge the gap during your attack without the advantage of throwing a combination (see opposite page), you have to position yourself in precisely the right place. And this, as Bruce wrote, is "often set up by readjusting the distance with footwork."[1] The push off, stealing step, and stutter step are all footwork tools that make this possible.

Because you've got to bridge the gap completely with only one move, this kind of attack is usually, though not always, implemented with the lead hand or leg, your closest tools to the target. Against left stancers, a single attack with a rear cross would also be a good choice. Whatever the weapon, when it comes to simple angle attacks, it's wise to follow Driscoll's advice—hit first, hit hard, hit often, and hit straight.[2]

ATTACK BY COMBINATION (ABC)

Just as its name implies, an attack by combination is a sequence of punches and/or kicks designed to create an opening. Usually this involves attacks thrown in different lines, but combinations can also be thrown in the same line as with double or triple leads. You can also throw combos in either different or identical lines with variations in tempo, depth, and cadence.

For any combination, the aim is to open up striking opportunities in a way that mechanically flows well to maximize speed and minimize energy expenditure. Here are examples of basic combinations thrown in different lines as listed by Bruce[3] and some notes on the mechanics for transitioning between techniques. You will find most of these combinations were taken directly from Haislet's book:[4]

1. **The one-two, otherwise known as the jab-cross.** Upon completion of the jab, I'm already looking at the target for the cross (Figure 15.2). For maximum speed, as you retract the jab, begin throwing the rear cross (Figure 15.3). Push off with your left foot to throw the jab, the right foot lands just after the jab makes contact with the target, and before your back foot lands you should have already made contact with the rear cross (Figure 15.4). If you are at a closer range and want to maximize speed, throw the jab more like a corkscrew with the palm down instead of a pure straight lead. Recover as you would with any other cross (Figure 15.4–15.5). You are now in a perfect position to throw a hook (Figure 15.6).

Figure 15.1

Figure 15.2

Figure 15.3

Figure 15.4

Figure 15.5

Figure 15.6

2. **The lead low/lead high.** Some examples of this would be a drop-shift/straight to the head (Figures 15.7–15.8), drop shift/hook to the head, hook to the body/hook to the head.

Figure 15.7

Figure 15.8

3. **Rear low/lead high.** Examples: drop shift/hook to head, drop shift/corkscrew to head (Figures 15.9–15.10).

Figure 15.9

Figure 15.10

4. **Lead low/rear high.** Try the lead low/overhand left—a boxing favorite (Figures 15.11–15.12).

Figure 15.11

Figure 15.12

5. **Rear high/lead low.** Example: rear cross/hook to body (Figures 15.13–15.14).

Figure 15.13

Figure 15.14

6. **One-two-three, otherwise known as the jab-cross-hook.** One of the most naturally flowing combinations, the jab-cross-hook is heavily dependent on footwork. The jab-cross portion is the same as for the one-two. After you've thrown the cross (Figure 15.15), your stance will be open. To move back into a safer position—the JKD stance—throw a hook (Figures 15.16–15.19).

Figure 15.15

Figure 15.16

Figure 15.17

Figure 15.18

Figure 15.19

7. **Jab/hook.** Also known in boxing circles as a hook-off-a-jab (Figures 15.20–15.27). The trick is in precise footwork and coordinated recovery (Figure 15.22). After impact, immediately relax the arm and retract the hip so that you can fire that hook ASAP. If your arm is at all tense during retraction, you'll be too slow—and tired—to pull off this combo. Other variations: jab/uppercut and jab/uppercut/hook (Figures 15.28–15.41). The latter is a great combo that bridges the gap with a jab, draws your opponent's defense in a low line, which allows you to land upstairs with a hook. With enough drilling, this can be a very fast, natural, and dangerous combo in your arsenal.

Figure 15.20

Figure 15.21

Figure 15.22

Figure 15.23

Figure 15.24

Figure 15.25

Figure 15.26

Hook-off-a-jab

Figure 15.27

Figure 15.28

Figure 15.29

Figure 15.30

Figure 15.31

Figure 15.32

Figure 15.33

Figure 15.34

Figure 15.35

Figure 15.36

Figure 15.37

Figure 15.38

Figure 15.39

Figure 15.40

Figure 15.41

Jab/Uppercut/Hook—It's all in the hips. As soon as I've finished the straight (Figure 15.30), I retract the hand with my hips first, which puts me in position for the uppercut (Figure 15.31). As always, I initiate the uppercut with the hip (Figure 15.33). Upon completion of the uppercut, I also retract immediately with the hip (Figure 15.36), which puts me right in position to throw the hook (Figure 15.37). Again, I lead with the hip and complete the hook (Figures 15.38–15.41). Remember for each punch, after impact, immediately relax the arm.

8. **Jab/rear hammer.** You can use this against a ducker. When he ducks your jab, nail him on the back of the neck. This is, of course, illegal in boxing and not something you want to do in sparring situations because of the injury risk (Figure 15.42).

Figure 15.42

9. **Jab/low cross/hook.** Used against a right stancer who pivots to his right. The low cross sets up a low left hook to the kidneys. Pivoting left temporarily puts you out of position with your left foot forward (Figure 15.44). To restore your stance, simply throw a rear cross with your strong hand—a haymaker—or a right hook. This pretty niftily places you right back into position. This also puts you in great position to deliver a left shovel hook to the kidney (Figure 15.45).

Figure 15.43

Figure 15.44

Figure 15.45

Depending on the range, you can also substitute hook kicks or elbows for hook punches.

Some people mistakenly think that because we practice combinations, we are learning set patterns. This is nonsense. Boxers practice combinations all the time, and no one would ever accuse them of fighting according to memorized patterns. Bruce Lee was one of the first fighters to train with focus mitts. At that time, their use was not common even among boxing trainers. Drilling in combinations brings you closer to the stage of Artlessness, where training and conditioning elicit an *appropriate* automatic response under pressure. Bruce used Haislet's explanation to explain the need for drilling:

> *"Conditioning is a process whereby a specific stimulus will cause a specific reaction. A repeated stimulus eventually creates an action pattern in the nervous system. Once this pattern is established the mere presence of the stimulus will cause a specific action. Such action is instantaneous and almost unconscious which is necessary for effective countering. In boxing, conditioned action should be the result of intense and concentrated practice of planned action patterns in response to every lead. Such action should be practiced slowly, for hours, days, and weeks, always in response to certain leads. Finally, the lead itself will automatically bring the right counter."[5, 6]*

IMMOBILIZATION ATTACK (IA)

As I mentioned in *The Straight Lead*, immobilization attack, also known as attack by force, is one of the few remnants remaining from wing chun. Over the years, the term IA has been usurped by those who mistakenly claim that JKD is merely glorified wing chun. It's important to remember that IA is not just trapping. It encompasses all immobilization techniques including arm bars, choke holds, joint locks, etc.

In order for any kind of IA to work, it's got to be simple. The idea is to pin one of your opponent's limbs so that he cannot use it to counter you. The two most common forms of immobilization attack in JKD are hand immobilization and leg obstruction.

The former is a pretty inefficient—and potentially dangerous—way to go about things. Most people trap first, hit later. If you know what you're doing on the timing and distance fronts, though, it's a heckuva lot faster to just hit the guy! Boom! You're in. You're out. If you trap first, this keeps you at a close range and your opponent may counter with another weapon—the other hand, a knee, etc. If you are going to trap, it should be secondary to a fast offensive. All that matters is that you land first. So punch first. Immobilizing the hand is just a precaution. And even then, it's a lot better to merely evade, because immobilization occupies your own hand, which could be put to better use as a weapon.

The other version of immobilization is leg obstruction. There is a distinction, though, between leg obstruction and an actual offensive kick. The latter is much more effective. It is a counter-offensive to a kick. Leg obstruction, on the other hand, is not all that practical, because you have to be very precise to block a leg with a foot. Our legs are much harder to control than our arms. And if you're dealing with someone who has very good form, it's not really useable, because his leg will come straight up bent at the knee. You won't be able to reach him! (Figure 15.46) You only have a good chance at leg obstruction with someone who's pretty slow and brings the leg up already extended, and this isn't going to be a very threatening kick anyway.

In either case, both leg and hand immobilizations are very *passive* ways of attack. You block first, hit later. It's the way of attack that is least congruent with the JKD principles of directness and simplicity.

Figure 15.46
***Immobilization attack**—Avoid this passive attack.*

PROGRESSIVE INDIRECT ATTACK (PIA)

Progressive indirect attack, also known as attack by fraud, is set up either by a feint, fake, or uncommitted offensive. The purpose is to gain both distance and time. When you throw a punch, real or fake, you gain distance. You bridge the gap. And if you're good, your opponent will react. This buys you time to take advantage of the opening line.[7, 8]

This is why Bruce wrote, "JKD is built on feints." It's how you get to your opponent. For PIA to work, though, you've got to establish that you are dangerous. You can use SAA to set up PIA. Because you must bridge the gap, the tools closest to your opponent are the most frequently used for PIA. Your opponent, then, must know that he can be tagged and unpleasantly so with either the straight lead or lead kicks. If you manage to hit him early on and establish your legitimacy, the rest is cake. Every time you feint, he's going to flinch, buying you time and distance.

The good ol' "one-two" is also a form of PIA. You might throw the jab with very little expectation of hitting your opponent. Still, throw it out there to bridge the gap. Then nail him with the cross. And if he's too slow to react to the first punch, hit him anyway! Keep in mind that when you fake, which is more of a committed move than a feint, you generally would not follow up with the same hand because you lose precious time having to retract that hand before throwing it out again. So if you fake a jab, follow up with the cross. If you fake a cross, follow up with the jab.

Varying the depth of your punches is another form of PIA. Move in deep to bridge the gap without the expectation that you will land the punch. Then follow up with a short punch. Don't forget that changes in speed, rhythm, and cadence can all be used for PIA. For example, you can throw a punch, stop, fake, and attack!

Some favorite examples of PIA—and you'll see these throughout Bruce's films—would be:

- fake straight lead/hook kick (Figures 15.47–15.48)

Figure 15.47   **Figure 15.48**

■ fake high/low straight lead (Figures 15.49–15.50)

Figure 15.49

Figure 15.50

■ drop shift/high straight lead
■ fake lead kick/straight lead
■ drop shift/high hook
■ short straight lead (may or may not land)/long straight lead
■ long straight lead (may or may not land)/short straight lead/short straight lead

ATTACK BY DRAWING (ABD)

Attack by drawing is our only form of *indirect* attack.[9] This means you make your opponent come to you. And this is where footwork is so important. You can set your man up by establishing a predictable pattern of rhythm and movement. For example, you can step back, step back, step back. He will follow you to maintain the fighting measure. And then suddenly on the half beat, wham! You move in and nail him. Footwork enables you to time your attack.

You can also invite an attack in a certain line, and judging from the distance, know which tools are available to him. For instance, you might keep your front hand down, virtually inviting him to take a swipe at you (Figures 15.51). With your hand down, though, you're inviting a high line attack. If you keep both hands up by the sides of your chin, you're inviting a low line shot to the solar plexus, an uppercut, or a straight up the middle. You can eliminate the possibility of a hook to either side of your head as a threat.

Another version of ABD is what fencing circles call 2nd intention or counter time. This is a counter-counter. You make a move causing your opponent to counter. You expect this counter and counter his counter. I know this is starting to sound like a Marx Brothers movie. Bear with me. For example, you throw a jab expecting a counter. When he gives this to you in the form of a jab, you counter his counter with a drop-shift or corkscrew. By the way, the low line reduces your target area, so the drop shift is a good choice if your stop thrust should fail.

Figure 15.51

Figure 15.52

Figure 15.53

Figure 15.54

Attack by drawing—*By keeping my lead hand low, I invite a highline attack (Figure 15.51). I set up a pattern by parrying twice (Figures 15.52 and 15.53) and then break that pattern with a drop-shift on the half-beat (Figure 15.54).*

ABD vs. PIA

It's important to know the distinction between ABD and PIA. A lot of instructors do not distinguish between the two, and they may often look identical, but it should be clear in your head what you are doing. Remember earlier we said there are two ways to see some action. Either your opponent comes to you or you go to him.

If you throw a kick, punch, or feint, you are taking the fight to him. This is PIA. Even if you feint, if you do so with the intention of creating an opening for attack, then it is a form of PIA.

If, on the other hand, you feint with the intention of making him counter so that he comes to you, then it is ABD. Your plan is to draw an offensive reaction out of him, so that you can counter him. The difference, then, is one of intention.

CHAPTER SIXTEEN

PARTING SHOTS: ON SELF-SUFFICIENCY

THE ART OF EXPRESSING THE HUMAN BODY

The bulk of this volume has consisted of technical instruction. This is, as we argued earlier, the Stage of Art, the meat and potatoes of any endeavor. But it's not enough to simply mimic the motions described throughout this book. It's not enough just to place your limbs in roughly the same positions as you see in the pictures. To truly master these techniques you are going to have to go one step further.

Once again, we look to Zen philosophy to give us a better understanding. Tokitsu gives a beautiful explanation of this in his book on Musashi:

> "The perfection of a gesture was derived from a kind of internalization; it was a matter of finding the total expression of the person within the limits dictated by his position. The idea was that nothing in the person making the gesture should remain outside or alienated from it. The gesture, a technical one or an ordinary gesture of daily life, was received as a total expression of the person making it."[1]

This is what Bruce Lee was referring to when he spoke of the "art of expressing the human body."[2] And it is with this mindset that you must approach even the smallest details of your training.

The absence of this mindset really is a fundamental flaw in our modern approach to so many things. I see it all the time in the fitness industry. Even if a group instructor or trainer does try to incorporate some mechanics, most people in their rushed lives won't take the time to hear what's being offered. So I see classrooms full of cardio kickboxers absent-mindedly flailing away at the air and on the bag. This is just another set of movements for them. In a few weeks, they'll grow tired of it and look for something else.

This is one reason why so many people fail in their fitness programs. They're bored out of their skulls trudging on a treadmill to nowhere. There is a huge, unnecessary and unnatural separation of mind and body today. If we would approach physical movement differently, if we would look beyond the surface of the gross movement and instead, seek to express ourselves through focused, skilled action, I have a sneaking suspicion we would be a lot less sedentary society.

The trouble is that from our first PE classes, we're not taught the necessity of body feel. From Day One, we're told what the movement looks like but we're never told what it should feel like. From throwing a football to swinging a baseball bat—we see the motion and then imitate. Those who are lucky instinctively feel it, and those who can't get left behind. I have a theory, though, that everyone can acquire a certain level of physical proficiency given the proper instruction and opportunity to "feel it out." That this doesn't happen is a shame, because there is a great deal of joy to be derived from being comfortable in our own skins. We are, after all, physical beings, and to deny ourselves this basic satisfaction of mastery over movement goes against nature.

Unfortunately, the absent-mindedness that pervades most physical instruction is also reflected in a lot of "JKD" instruction. Book after book, video after video—I see a lot of people mimicking the photos in Bruce Lee's *Fighting Method* series. Even in still photos—by their foot position, their center of gravity, the tension in their arms—you can see that they have not acquired the necessary body feel. It is, as Bruce would call it "surface knowledge." And in their actual movement, they are lacking the fluidity and concentration of energy that would demonstrate a real understanding of the art.

As Bruce himself wrote, "Real knowledge breeds 'body feel' and personal expression."[3] Throughout his writings, you will see that Bruce repeatedly emphasized the importance of body feel.[4] To enable you to cultivate "real knowledge" and avoid the pitfalls of "surface knowledge," then, I ask that you take special care in your training to *be present*. When you practice and, even more importantly, when you are learning a new technique, be *aware*. Don't just go through the motions and move on.

Even with something as simple as standing in the stance, be aware of how it *feels*. Can you feel the potential energy stored on the medial sides of your legs? How all that energy is concentrated in the ball of your left foot? Can you feel the ground beneath you and how ground reaction force will propel you into motion? How a slight shift forward would give you that little bit of extra explosiveness into the push off? Or how lowering your center of gravity allows you to hunker down with more stability?

Strive to know that stance so well that when you are not in it, your *body* will know. Obviously there will be times in a fight, when you are constantly in motion, when you will be temporarily out of position. You'll practice how to deal with this as well. The point is that the more aware you are of how all your body parts relate to each other based on their position in space, the more adaptability you'll have.

BODY FEEL EXERCISES

"Study body feel," Bruce instructed, "to get speed, fluidity, and power."[5] For fluidity, of course, shadowboxing is the best exercise. You aren't going for power here. Instead get a feel for how to transition from one technique to the next. Maintain balance over a constantly shifting base of support. Watch yourself in the mirror. Ask yourself how you'd handle a particular situation. Then see how your body reacts. Be light, shifty.

According to Ted Wong, there is one exercise Bruce practiced to develop control and focused power. It can be used for any technique. Essentially, you are air kicking or air punching. Normally at the end of a punch or kick, you would reach full extension and then snap back into the on-guard position. In this case, though, you'll stop yourself in mid-air at what would normally be the point of impact. You do so with all the force of your most powerful punch, and you should feel that energy concentrated at the end of your bottom three knuckles.

The analogy that Bruce would use is that of a water hose or a water bottle. If you were to take a partially filled water bottle and go through the motion of throwing it like a football, without letting it go, at the end of the motion, you'd feel all the water jerk from one end of the bottle to the other end. That's the same concentration of force you should feel at the end of your punch.

This is much more difficult than actually hitting something. You can fudge it when you have a target. The resistance gives you something to bounce off of. But to stop your self mid-air, with the same force you would direct at a target requires a great deal of control. For example, if you're practicing a hook kick, you throw out that kick with all the intensity and snap as you normally would but stop at the point of imagined impact. Your instep should stop on a dime. No adjustments, no disruption of balance, no dangling foot. Everything focused on the point of impact.

This is also a great drill for practicing fakes and feints. It's got to be convincing so you have to throw a fake with the same intensity as the real thing but with the control to stop short at any point. You should be able to stop on a dime with full-out intensity at any point during a technique—at full extension, at partial extension, at the shoulder only. That's controlled power, and you get it through body feel.

GOOD FORM

For all this talk of body feel, of course, the natural question is, "What should I be feeling?" This is where good form and biomechanics come in. In the realm of body feel, I can only take you so far. You've got to put in the work of actually, well, feeling it for yourself. Or as Zen masters would say, you must *experience* it. But what I can do is give you the proper form and mechanics that go with each technique, a sort of mental checklist to go through that will point you in the right direction—hence, the purpose of this volume.

The importance of good form cannot be overemphasized. It is the foundation of *everything*. Under the "Good Form" section in the *Tao*, Bruce wrote, "The mastery of proper fundamentals and their progressive application is the secret of being a great fighter."[6] You cannot be a great fighter without a solid foundation.

To help you understand the things you should be looking out for, refer back to the chapter on biomechanics so that each point won't look like a mere laundry list of things to remember. Each technical point has a purpose.

For example, in the chapter on hook punching, I'm not telling you to move the hip first just to make you crazy. The hip moves first so that you'll feel a catch on your shoulder. That catch, or extra tension, gives you more potential energy at the shoulder. We examined this concept of strain energy in the biomechanics chapter. With this extra knowledge, then, you know what the checkpoints are for each technique. When you go to practice your hook, you're aware of what you should be feeling at the shoulder joint and why.

Why all the fuss over these checkpoints? Because skipping them leads to bad habits, and bad habits are hard to reprogram. Bad habits will slow you down. Bad habits lead to cumulative injury cycles. And bad habits, with their telegraphic tendencies and extraneous movement, can also get you in a pickle. The human body is the most complex piece of machinery in the world. Kinesthetic perception (body feel) involves the gathering of information from Golgi tendon organs, muscle spindles, alpha and gamma neurons, and the nervous system, as well as all other sources of afferent data.

And then to react to this information, you must develop the proper response through a complex process of neuromuscular programming.[7] The point is you cannot skip steps, as Rasch and Burke explain:

> *"It is a matter of common observation that a child stands before he walks and walks before he runs. Complex motor learning requires an order of prerequisites, a background of specific attainments. Complex coordinations cannot be mastered until certain basic movement patterns have been reduced to the automaticity of conditioned reflexes. In general, fine movements are distilled out of gross movements; new skills are based upon recombinations of old skills."[8]*

To reach your full potential, then, you need to build a solid foundation first. Consider this book as the basis for building that foundation. "The chief consideration in developing form," Bruce wrote, "is to make sure that *no fundamental, mechanical principles are violated*."[9] This book has been about providing the instruction for each technique so that no biomechanical principles are violated.

ON SELF-SUFFICIENCY

The point of giving you the mechanics of each technique in such detail and the physical laws behind them is to make you self-sufficient. If something's gone wrong with one of your weapons, or if you're just looking to get yourself to the next level, eventually, you should be able to take the information here and fix it yourself. Too many of us look to external sources for the answers. We think the answer lies in another art, with another teacher, with different techniques. No. These are the very marketing ploys that Musashi was on to even during his time.

Nor does the answer lie in exotic, mystical powers. "Don't look for secret moves," Bruce wrote. "Don't look for secret movements. If you're always hunting for secret techniques you're going to miss it. It's you. It's your body that's the key."[10]

It has nothing to do with race or Eastern religion. It's pure discipline and persistence in the *physical* world, and adherence to laws of a physical world, that lead to the kind of personal power that has been mistaken as mysticism. It's the kind of devotion, self-exploration, and self-reliance, day in and day out, with all of our distinctly human physical and mental limitations, that puts us in touch with all that is good, truthful, and transcendent.

NOTES

Author's Note

1 Ted Wong with John Little, *Bruce Lee's Lead Punch: Ted Wong explains Jun Fan Jeet Kune Do's Most Explosive Technique!* June, 2000, pp. 58. According to John Little the actual number of meetings between Bruce Lee and Ted Wong may be much higher than 122.

2 Bruce Lee, ed. John Little, *Jeet Kune Do: Bruce Lee's Commentaries on the Martial Way* (Boston: Tuttle Publishing, 1997), p. 14.

Introduction: The Necessity of Technique

1 Bruce Lee, ed. John Little, *Jeet Kune Do: Bruce Lee's Commentaries on the Martial Way* (Boston: Tuttle Publishing, 1997), p. 298.

2 Bruce Lee, *Tao of Jeet Kune Do* (Santa Clarita: Ohara Publications, Inc. 1997), p. 200.

3 Daisets T. Suzuki, *Zen and Japanese Culture* (Princeton: Princeton University Press, 1959), p. 121.
   "The swordsman's mind must be kept entirely free from selfish affects and intellectual calculations so that 'original intuition' is ready to work at its best—which is a state of no-mind-ness…He must once realize the final stage of spiritual discipline, which is to attain no-mind-ness, symbolized as a circle empty of contents—a circle with no circumference."

4 Bruce Lee, ed. John Little, *Bruce Lee: Artist of Life* (Boston: Tuttle Publishing, 1999), p. 165.

5 Lee, ed. John Little, *Jeet Kune Do: Bruce Lee's Commentaries on the Martial Way*, p. 341.

6 Suzuki, *Zen and Japanese Culture*, p 104.

7 Lee, *Tao of Jeet Kune Do*, p. 7–9. This section is actually entitled "On Zen" and most of these statements can be found in classics of Zen literature.

8 Suzuki, *Zen and Japanese Culture*, p. 104

9 Lee, ed. John Little, *Bruce Lee: Artist of Life*, p. 165.

10 Ibid., p. 160.

11 Lee, ed. John Little, *Jeet Kune Do: Bruce Lee's Commentaries on the Martial Way*, p. 255.

12 Kenji Tokitsu, *Miyamoto Musashi: His Life and Writings* (Boston: Weatherhill, 2004), p. 189.

13 From Bruce Lee's personal notes.

14 Suzuki, *Zen and Japanese Culture*, p. 99.

15 Lee, ed. John Little, *Jeet Kune Do: Bruce Lee's Commentaries on the Martial Way*, p. 353.

16 Suzuki, *Zen and Japanese Culture*, p. 99.

17 Suzuki, *Zen and Japanese Culture*, p. 95.

18 Lee, ed. John Little, *Jeet Kune Do: Bruce Lee's Commentaries on the Martial Way*, p. 61.

19 Lee, ed. John Little, *Bruce Lee: Artist of Life*, p. 165.

20 Roger Crosnier, *Fencing and the Foil: Instruction and Technique* (London: Faber and Faber, 1948), p. 63. Bruce directly quotes Crosier. See next note.

21 Lee, ed. John Little, *Jeet Kune Do: Bruce Lee's Commentaries on the Martial Way*, p. 255.

22 Suzuki, *Zen and Japanese Culture*, p. 31.

Chapter 1: Biomechanics 101

1 Peter M. McGinnis, *Biomechanics of Sport and Exercise 2nd Edition*, (Champaign: Human Kinetics, 2005), p. 48–49.

2 Paul G. Hewitt, *Conceptual Physics 9th Edition* (San Francisco: Addison Wesley, 2002), p. 772.

3 Bruce Lee, *Tao of Jeet Kune Do* (Santa Clarita: Ohara Publications, Inc., 1975), p. 58.

4 Bruce Lee, ed. John Little, *The Tao of Gung Fu* (Boston: Tuttle Publishing, 1997), p. 211.

5 McGinnis, *Biomechanics of Sport and Exercise 2nd Edition*, p. 64–70.

6 Ibid., p. 73.

7 Ibid., p. 106.

8 Jack Dempsey, *Championship Fighting: Explosive Punching and Aggressive Defense* (New York: Prentice Hall, Inc., 1950), p. 29.

9 McGinnis, *Biomechanics of Sport and Exercise 2nd Edition*, p. 107.

10 Lee, *Tao of Jeet Kune Do*, p. 58.

11 McGinnis, *Biomechanics of Sport and Exercise 2nd Edition*, p. 109. There's a great explanation of how the shot putting technique evolved to maximize shot displacement prior to release.

12 Hewitt, *Conceptual Physics 9th Edition*. p. 27.

13 Lee, *Tao of Jeet Kune Do*, p. 49.

14 Gerry Carr, *Sport Mechanics for Coaches 2nd Edition*, (Champaign: Human Kinetics, 2004), p. 77–78.

15 Lee, *Tao of Jeet Kune Do*, p. 58.

16 Ibid., p. 108.

17 Bruce Lee, ed. John Little, *Jeet Kune Do: Bruce Lee's Commentaries on the Martial Way* (Boston: Tuttle Publishing, 1997), p. 385.

18 Hewitt, *Conceptual Physics 9th Edition*, p. 134.

19 Carr, *Sport Mechanics for Coaches 2nd Edition*, p. 102-103.

20 Lee, ed. John Little, *Jeet Kune Do: Bruce Lee's Commentaries on the Martial Way*, p. 201.

21 McGinnis, *Biomechanics of Sport and Exercise 2nd Edition*, p. 137–142.

22 Carr, *Sport Mechanics for Coaches 2nd Edition*, p. 107–108.

23 McGinnis, *Biomechanics of Sport and Exercise 2nd Edition*, p. 95.

Chapter 2: The Stance

1 Teri Tom, *The Straight Lead: The Core of Bruce Lee's Jun Fan Jeet Kune Do* (North Clarendon: Tuttle Publishing, 2006), p. 50–56.

2 Bruce Lee, *Tao of Jeet Kune Do* (Santa Clarita: Ohara Publications, Inc., 1975), p. 144.

3 Bruce Lee, ed. John Little, *Jeet Kune Do: Bruce Lee's Commentaries on the Martial Way* (Boston: Tuttle Publishing, 1997), p. 156

4 Lee, ed John Little, *Jeet Kune Do: Bruce Lee's Commentaries on the Martial Way*, p. 191.

5 Lee, *Tao of Jeet Kune Do*, p. 146

6 Thomas Inch, *Boxing: The Secret of the Knockout*, (Kingswood: The World's Work, LTD., 1913), p. 18.

Chapter 3: Footwork

1 Bruce Lee, *Tao of Jeet Kune Do* (Santa Clarita: Ohara Publications, Inc., 1975), p. 145.

2 Vijay Prashad, "Summer of Bruce" in *Screaming Monkeys* (Minneapolis: Coffee House Press), p. 256. Prashad writes,
   "In an instance of classic cross-fertilization, the great boxer Sugar Ray Leonard told an interviewer in 1982 that 'one of the guys who influenced me wasn't a boxer. I always loved the catlike reflexes and the artistry of Bruce Lee and I wanted to do in boxing what he was able to do in karate [sic]. I started watching his movies before he became really popular in Enter the Dragon *and I patterned myself after a lot of his ways.'"*

3 Bruce Lee, ed. John Little, *Jeet Kune Do: Bruce Lee's Commentaries on the Martial Way* (Boston: Tuttle Publishing, 1997), p. 93.

4 Ibid., p. 65–66.

5 Ibid., p. 193.

6 Lee, *Tao of Jeet Kune Do*, p. 142. Lee writes:
   "The quality of a man's technique depends on his footwork, for one cannot use his hands or kicks efficiently until his feet have put him in the desired position."
   Compare to footnote 7.

7 Bobby Neill, *Instruction to Young Boxers* (London: Museum Press Limited, 1961), 13. Sounding very similar to the above footnote, Bruce Lee had underlined the following passage from Neill's book:
   "You cannot use your hands efficiently until your feet have put you into a position in which you can do so. Your feet are your foundation…"

8 Lee, *Tao of Jeet Kune Do*, p. 144.

9 Ibid., p. 152. Bruce makes a similar reference to the stance:
   "Remember also to always retain the fundamental stance. No matter what you do with that moving pedestal, the turret carrying the artillery must remain well poised, a constant threat to your foe. Aim always to move fluidly but retain the relative position of the two feet."

10 Ibid., p. 145–147.

11 Ibid., p. 147:
"Lighten the stance so the force of inertia to be overcome will be less."

12 Lee, *Tao of Jeet Kune Do*, p. 148. Taken verbatim from Haislet. See next note.

13 Edwin L. Haislet, *Boxing* (New York: A.S. Barnes & Noble Company, 1940), p. 31.

14 Ibid., p. 32:
"This forward advance of the body without disturbing the body balance which can only be performed through a series of short steps forward. These steps must be so small that the feet are not lifted at all, but slide along the floor."

15 Lee, *Tao of Jeet Kune Do*, p. 148.

16 Haislet, *Boxing*, p. 34. Taken directly from Haislet on p. 148 of the *Tao*.

17 Jack Dempsey, *Championship Fighting: Explosive Punching and Aggressive Defense* (New York: Prentice Hall, Inc., 1950), p. 60:
"Move first the foot closest to the direction you wish to go in. In other words, if you wish to sidestep to the left, move the left foot first and vice versa."
A similar note can be found in the *Tao*. See note below.

18 Lee, *Tao of Jeet Kune Do*, p. 152.

19 Ibid., p. 151.

20 Haislet, *Boxing*, p. 97:
"The sidestep was made for the rusher. As the opponent rushes, sidestep and deliver a counterblow."
Compare to the *Tao*. See next note.

21 Lee, *Tao of Jeet Kune Do*, p. 150.

22 Haislet, *Boxing*, p. 97:
"The right lead leg becomes a movable pivot that wheels the whole body to the right until the correct position is resumed. The first step with the right foot be as short or as long as necessary—the longer the step, the greater the pivot. The fundamental position must be maintained at all times."
Quoted directly in the *Tao*. See note below.

23 Lee, *Tao of Jeet Kune Do*, p. 149.

24 Aldo Nadi, *On Fencing*, (Bangor: Laureate Press, 1994), p. 51.

25 Lee, ed. John Little, *Jeet Kune Do: Bruce Lee's Commentaries on the Martial Way*, p. 193.

26 Ibid., p. 193.

Chapter 4: The Straight Lead

1 Edwin L. Haislet, *Boxing* (New York: A.S. Barnes & Noble Company, 1940), p. 7.

2 Bruce Lee and M. Uyehara, *Bruce Lee's Fighting Method: Basic Training* (Burbank: Ohara Publications, Inc.), p. 33.

3 Clark and Corn, *NASM Optimum Performance Training for the Fitness Professional*, p. 104.

4 Ibid., p. 106.

5 Aldo Nadi, *On Fencing*, (Bangor, ME: Laureate Press, 1994), p. 89.

6 Lee, *Tao of Jeet Kune Do* (Santa Clarita, CA, Ohara Publications, Inc., 1975), p. 97.

7 Teri Tom, *The Straight Lead: The Core of Bruce Lee's Jun Fan Jeet Kune Do* (North Clarendon: Tuttle Publishing, 2006), p. 36.

8 Lee, *Bruce Lee's Fighting Method: Basic Training*, p. 74.

9 Jack Dempsey, *Championship Fighting: Explosive Punching and Aggressive Defense* (New York: Prentice Hall, Inc., 1950), p. 34. The following passage was underlined in Bruce Lee's copy:
"The power line runs from either shoulder—straight down the length of the arm—to the FIRST KNUCKLE OF THE LITTLE FINGER, when the fist is doubled. You might call that pinky knuckle the exit of your power line—the muzzle of your cannon."
For a fuller explanation of the Power Line, please see the chapter on the JFJD stance in *The Straight Lead*.

10 Bruce Lee, ed, John Little, *The Tao of Gung Fu* (Boston: Tuttle Publishing, 1997), p. 211.

11 Haislet, *Boxing*, p. 26.

12 Ibid., p. 16.

13 Lee, *Tao of Jeet Kune Do*, p. 88.

14 Bruce Lee, ed. John Little, *Jeet Kune Do: Bruce Lee's Commentaries on the Martial Way* (Boston: Tuttle Publishing, 1997), p. 210.

15 Ibid., p. 210.

Chapter 5: Variations of the Straight Lead

1 Bruce Lee, *Tao of Jeet Kune Do* (Santa Clarita: Ohara Publications, Inc. 1975), p. 112:
"When you step in with the corkscrew, you move in with a 'pivot step'—stepping forward and slightly to your own right, pointing the toe sharply in. Your body pivots on the ball of your right foot as your right arm and fist snap down to the target. At the instant of the fist's landing, your rear left foot generally is in the air, but it settles immediately behind you."
You'll find this exact passage in Dempsey's book. See next note.

2 Jack Dempsey, *Championship Fighting: Explosive Punching and Aggressive Defense* (New York: Prentice Hall, Inc., 1950), pp. 97–98.

3 Lee, *Tao of Jeet Kune Do*, p. 112. Taken from Dempsey. See note below.

4 Dempsey, *Championship Fighting: Explosive Punching and Aggressive Defense*, p. 95:
"The corkscrew usually is a medium range punch, and [is] usually delivered while you are circling to your opponent's right."

5 Lee, *Tao of Jeet Kune Do*, p. 112:
"If he permits his guarding left hand to creep too far forward as he blocks or parries your right jab, your corkscrew can snap down behind that guarding left and nail his jaw."
Passage taken verbatim from Dempsey. See note below.

6 Dempsey, *Championship Fighting: Explosive Punching and Aggressive Defense*, p. 96.

7 Lee, *Tao of Jeet Kune Do*, p. 110:
"Shovel hooks are thrown 'inside' with the elbows in, pressing tightly against the hips for body blows and pressing tightly against the lower ribs for head blows."
Taken directly from Dempsey. See note below.

8 Dempsey, *Championship Fighting: Explosive Punching and Aggressive Defense*, p. 83.

9 Lee, *Tao of Jeet Kune Do*, p. 110. Taken directly from Dempsey. See below.

10 Dempsey, *Championship Fighting: Explosive Punching and Aggressive Defense*, p. 85.

11 Lee, *Tao of Jeet Kune Do*, p. 111. Taken directly from Dempsey. See below.

12 Dempsey, *Championship Fighting: Explosive Punching and Aggressive Defense*, p. 89.

13 Bruce Lee, ed. John Little, *Jeet Kune Do: Bruce Lee's Commentaries on the Martial Way* (Boston: Tuttle Publishing, 1997), p. 196. Here you'll find Bruce's comments on side-stepping in conjunction with the drop shift. We'll return to this passage when we discuss the rear cross.

Chapter 6: The Rear Cross

1 From Bruce Lee's handwritten notes.

2 Bruce Lee, *Tao of Jeet Kune Do* (Santa Clarita: Ohara Publications, Inc., 1975), p. 103. Bruce stressed the importance of footwork and where it puts you *after* you've thrown the cross. Unless you have *correct* balance, you will not be in a position to deliver a lead shot after your rear cross. This is most important, because if your opponent ducks to avoid the rear cross, your *quickest method of recovery* is to throw a lead and you must be in a correct position to do so. If you are trying to correct faulty footwork in those split seconds, you may well find yourself flat on your back.

3 Bruce Lee, ed. John Little, *Jeet Kune Do: Bruce Lee's Commentaries on the Martial Way* (Boston: Tuttle Publishing, 1997), p. 233. Bruce describes the weight transfer:
"Press down on the ball of the right foot, and you must control the forward movement transferring the weight from the left to right foot before connecting. Your left foot should follow by dragging it forward."

4 Lee, *Tao of Jeet Kune Do*, p. 102. Bruce cites the additional hip rotation as the main reason why the rear cross is a power shot:
"The rear cross is delivered in much the same manner as the lead jab in that it travels in a perfectly straight line. The rear cross, however, is the heavy artillery and the twist at your waist will be much greater."

5 Lee, *Tao of Jeet Kune Do*, p. 102

6 Ibid., p. 105. According to Bruce:
"The overhand left is used by small fellows against taller men. It travels in a circular and over motion into the vicinity of the opposition's head. The movement must come from the shoulder (vary it with an inward palm strike)."

7 Lee, ed. John Little, *Jeet Kune Do: Bruce Lee's Commentaries on the Martial Way*, p. 196.

8 Ibid., p. 196. Also on the drop shift:
"The drop shift—is a further refinement of the side step. It is used to gain the inside or outside guard position and is useful in in-fighting. Mainly a vehicle for countering it requires timing-speed, and judgment to properly execute. It may be combined with the right jab, the straight left, the left hook, and the right hook."

Chapter 7: The Hook

1 Bruce Lee, ed. John Little, *Jeet Kune Do: Bruce Lee's Commentaries on the Martial Way* (Boston: Tuttle Publishing, 1997), p. 223.

2 Bruce Lee, *Tao of Jeet Kune Do* (Santa Clarita: Ohara Publications, Inc., 1975), p. 108:
"The lead heel must be raised outward so that the body can pivot, and the waist and shoulders reverse when the blow lands."

3 Thomas Inch, *Boxing: The Secret of the Knock-Out* (Kingswood: The World's Work, LTD, 1913), p.22.

4 Lee, ed. John Little, *Jeet Kune Do: Bruce Lee's Commentaries on the Martial Way* p. 225

5 Lee, *Tao of Jeet Kune Do*, p. 107:
"The hook is a good punch to combine with a sidestep, for you are moving sideways and it is the natural way to swing at that moment."

6 Edwin L. Haislet, *Boxing* (New York: A.S. Barnes & Noble Company, 1940), p. 8. In his explanation of leverage, Haislet similarly notes that the arm must follow the rest of the body:
"Arm action alone is insufficient to give real power to blows. Real power, quick and accurate, can be obtained only by shifting the weight in such a manner that the hip and shoulder precede the arm to the center line of the body."

7 Lee, *Tao of Jeet Kune Do*, p. 108.

8 Ibid., p. 109:
"The more you 'open' an outside hook, the more it degenerates into a swing. You must keep it tight. Also, when you open a hook, you open your own defense."
Taken directly from Dempsey. See note below.

9 Jack Dempsey, *Championship Fighting: Explosive Punching and Aggressive Defense* (New York: Prentice Hall, Inc., 1950), p. 89.

10 Lee, *Tao of Jeet Kune Do*, p. 109.
"At the finish of the punch, the thumb is up. There is no twist of the fist—for proper protection of the hand. The forearm is rigid from the elbow to the knuckles and does not bend at the wrist."

Chapter 8: The Uppercut

1 Bruce Lee, *Tao of Jeet Kune Do* (Santa Clarita: Ohara Publications, Inc., 1975), p. 113.

2 Thomas Inch, *Boxing: The Secret of the Knock-Out* (Kingswood: The World's Work, LTD, 1913), pp. 137 and 72. Compare *Tao* passage to two passages from Inch: "…leverage through first bending the legs and slightly leaning backwards" and "Legs should be bent before using this blow, straighten them as you send the punch in. Get up on your toes as the blow lands."

3 Ibid., p. 114:
"Screw the blow up and in so that you can send it to the chin."

4 From Bruce Lee's personal notes:
"More weight upon the left let when using the right and more upon the right leg when using the left uppercut."

5 Lee, *Tao of Jeet Kune Do*, p. 113.

6 From Bruce Lee's personal notes.

Chapter 9: Evasion

1 Bruce Lee, *Tao of Jeet Kune Do* (Santa Clarita: Ohara Publications, Inc., 1975), p. 143

2 Ibid., p. 154.

3 Ibid., p. 156: Taken directly from McInnes. See below.

4 Peter McInnes, *Tackle Boxing This Way* (London: Stanley Paul, 1960), p. 77:
"Few people realize that the real key to the successful slipping of blows lies in a little movement of the heel. If it is desired to slip a lead to the left so that it passes over the right shoulder the right heel should be lifted and twisted outwards.

This transfers the weight on to the left foot and twists the shoulders, setting the defender nicely to counter."

5 Bruce Lee, ed. John Little, *Jeet Kune Do: Bruce Lee's Commentaries on the Martial Way* (Boston: Tuttle Publishing, 1997), p. 168.

6 Lee, *Tao of Jeet Kune Do*, p. 158.

7 Ibid., p. 156. The exact passage in the *Tao* regarding ducking is taken directly from Haislet's book. See below.

8 Edwin L. Haislet, *Boxing* (New York: A.S. Barnes & Noble Company, 1940), pp. 49–50:
"Ducking is dropping forward under hooks and swings to the head. It is used as a means of escaping blows allowing the boxer to remain in range for a counter-attack. Neither ducking, slipping, nor weaving should be practiced without hitting or countering. It is just as necessary to learn to duck swings as it is to slip straight punches. Both are used for the same purpose, and both are important in counter-attack."

9 Ibid., p. 157.

10 Ibid., p. 158.

11 Ibid., p. 157.

12 Ibid., p. 157.

13 Ibid., p. 157.

14 Ibid., p. 134.

15 Ibid., p. 132:
"To reach out to parry a blow not only makes openings for counter-blows, but also enables the opponent to change the direction of his blow. Remember, parry late rather than early."

16 Ibid., p. 133. Taken directly from Crosnier. See below.

17 Roger Crosnier, *Fencing with the Foil* (London: Faber and Faber, 1948), p. 90:
"Semicircular parries are those taken from a high line of engagement to deflect an attack directed in the low line, or from a low line engagement to a high line. They describe a half-circle."

18 Ibid., p. 133.

Chapter 11: Advanced Footwork

1 Teri Tom, *The Straight Lead: The Core of Bruce Lee's Jun Fan Jeet Kune Do* (North Clarendon: Tuttle Publishing, 2006), pp. 93–94. The irony is that, as I noted in *The Straight Lead*, Bruce Lee's own influences, Jim Driscoll, Nadi, and Dempsey all complained about the lack of emphasis given to footwork in instruction.

2 Aldo Nadi, *On Fencing* (Bangor: Laureate Press, 1994), p. 183. Nadi claimed that the entire science of all fighting is based on the half beat:
"Actually, these "paradoxes" are the basis upon which the entire art and science of arms is built. In combat, when the fencer forsakes the orthodox attack and parry-riposte for the counterattack, he literally puts the half-note into the music of fencing, superimposing it upon, or obliterating temporarily, the whole-note concept and value. In fact, the stronger the fencer the greater the importance of, and the results obtained, by this half-note."

3 Bruce Lee, *Tao of Jeet Kune Do* (Santa Clarita: Ohara Publications, Inc., 1975), p. 62. Passage taken directly from Castello. See below.

4 Julio Martinez Castello, *The Theory and Practice of Fencing* (New York: Charles Scribner's Sons, 1933), pp. 56–57:
"Timing consists of selecting the opportune moment for making an attack or a parry. This opportune moment usually has to be created rather than discovered…The movements of the attacking and defending blades work almost in rhythm with each other, and although there is a slight advantage in the initiative of the attack, it must also be backed by superior speed in order to land successfully. However, when this rhythm is broken, speed is no longer the primary element in the success of the attack or counter attack of the man who has broken the rhythm."

5 Lee, *Tao of Jeet Kune Do*, pg. 125

6 Bruce Lee, ed. John Little, *Jeet Kune Do: Bruce Lee's Commentaries on the Martial Way* (Boston: Tuttle Publishing, 1997), p. 202. Don't be like the "fancy boxer" who is only "amusing himself"!

7 Lee, *Tao of Jeet Kune Do*, p. 149.

Chapter 12: Speed

1 Michael A. Clark and Rodney J. Corn, *NASM Sports Fitness Specialist Manual* (Calabasas: National Academy of Sports Medicine, 2002), IX–2

2 Bruce Lee, *Tao of Jeet Kune Do* (Santa Clarita, CA, Ohara Publications, Inc., 1975), p. 55.

3 Ibid., p. 55.

4 Ibid., p. 57.

5 Ibid., p. 57

6 Philip J. Rasch, *Kinesiology and Applied Anatomy* (Philadelphia, PA, Lea and Febiger, 1989), p. 74:
   "Complex coordinations cannot be mastered until certain basic movement patterns have been reduced to he automaticity of conditioned reflexes."

7 Clark and Corn, Corn, *NASM Sports Fitness Specialist Manual*, p. IX–9

8 Lee, *Tao of Jeet Kune Do*, p. 57.

9 Ibid., p. 57.

10 Ibid., p. 54–55.

11 In a conversation with Ted Wong, 2006.

12 Lee, *Tao of Jeet Kune Do*, p. 59.

Chapter 13: Hand and Feet Combinations

1 Bruce Lee, *Tao of Jeet Kune Do* (Santa Clarita: Ohara Publications, Inc., 1975), p. 173.

2 Ibid., p. 173

Chapter 14: Towards Application

1 Bruce Lee, *Tao of Jeet Kune Do* (Santa Clarita, CA, Ohara Publications, Inc., 1975), p. 163.

2 Ibid., p. 163:
   "A fighter who is observant will not carry on stubbornly with strokes that are no longer the right ones. So many fighters put down the failure of an offensive stroke to a lack of speed rather than to the incorrect choice of stroke. The pro knows better."

3 Ibid., p139. Taken directly from Crosnier. See below.

4 Roger Crosnier, *Fencing with the Foil* (London: Faber and Faber, 1948), p. 39.

5 Ibid., p. 148. Crosnier's notes on attacks on preparation can provide some insight into Bruce's incorporation of it into JFJKD:
   "During preparation the fencer increases his vulnerability firstly because he is clear to his opponent; secondly because his mind is usually concentrating on his offensive action as a whole; and thirdly, because of the obvious reason that he cannot simultaneously, step forward and backward."

6 Ibid., pp. 157–161. Crosnier's notes on the stop-hit.

7 Lee, *Tao of Jeet Kune Do*, p. 162.

8 Simon Frith, *Performing Rites: On the Value of Popular Music* (Cambridge: Harvard University Press, 1996), pp. 145–147.

9 Julio Martinez Castello, *The Theory and Practice of Fencing* (New York: Charles Scribner's Sons, 1933), pp. 56–57.

10 Lee, *Tao of Jeet Kune Do*, p. 62.

11 Ibid., p. 125

12 Ibid., p. 125:
   "He gains distance by starting his lunge with his feint and, simultaneously, gains time by deceiving the parry."

13 Ibid., p. 126.

14 Teri Tom, *The Straight Lead: The Core of Bruce Lee's Jun Fan Jeet Kune Do* (North Clarendon: Tuttle Publishing, 2006), p. 168.

15 Bruce Lee, ed. John Little, *Jeet Kune Do: Bruce Lee's Commentaries on the Martial Way* (Boston: Tuttle Publishing, 1997), p. 115.

16 Lee, Tao of Jeet Kune Do, p. 127:
   "By 'long' we do not mean slow. While penetrating deeply toward the opponent the feint must be fast. The combination of speed and penetration are the factors which draw the desired reaction from the defense."

Chapter 15: Application: The Five Ways of Attack

1 Bruce Lee, *Tao of Jeet Kune Do* (Santa Clarita, CA, Ohara Publications, Inc., 1975), p. 194.

2 Jim Driscoll, *The Straight Left and How to Cultivate It* (London: Athletic Publications, Ltd), p. 80.

3 Bruce Lee, ed. John Little, *Jeet Kune Do: Bruce Lee's Commentaries on the Martial Way* (Boston: Tuttle Publishing, 1997), p. 120–122.

4 Edwin L. Haislet, *Boxing* (New York: A.S. Barnes & Noble Company, 1940), pp. 88–93.

5 Lee, *Tao of Jeet Kune Do*, p. 177. Almost the exact same passage from Haislet's book can be found in the *Tao*.

6 Haislet, *Boxing*, p. 73.

7 Lee, *Tao of Jeet Kune Do*, p. 125:
   "He gains distance by starting his lunge with his feint and, simultaneously, gains time by deceiving the parry (the opponent's reaction) on the way to his target."
   This passage was clearly taken from Crosnier. See below.

8 Roger Crosnier, *Fencing with the Foil* (London: Faber and Faber, 1948), p. 130. The following passage was underlined by Bruce:
   "The advantage of a feint, or feints, must be that the attacker can start lunging with his feint and thus be gaining distance from the outset. He will have shortened the distance his point had to travel by a good half with his feint, and leave to his second movement only the second half of the distance. Thus he is at the same time gaining distance by starting his lunge with his feint, and simultaneously gaining time by deceiving the parry while doing so. The attack from the beginning is progressing towards the opponent, and for that reason is known as a progressive attack."

9 Ibid., pp. 61–63. Crosnier's notes on indirect attacks.

Chapter 16: Parting Shots: On Self-Sufficiency

1 Kenji Tokitsu, *Miyamoto Musashi: His Life and Writings* (Boston: Weatherhill, 2004), p. 287.

2 Bruce Lee, ed. John Little, *Jeet Kune Do:Bruce Lee's Commentaries on the Martial Way* (Boston: Tuttle Publishing, 1997), p. 34.

3 Ibid., p. 385.

4 Ibid., p. 146, 149, 154, 156, 172, 174, 182, 385.

5 Ibid., p. 156.

6 Bruce Lee, *Tao of Jeet Kune Do* (Santa Clarita: Ohara Publications, Inc. 1997), p. 53.

7 Lee, ed. John Little, *Jeet Kune Do: Bruce Lee's Commentaries on the Martial Way*, p. 26:
   "Acquire the kinesthetic perception in tension-creating situations—distinguish between the relaxed and the tense states. Practice controlling the body responses voluntarily and at will. Use only those muscles required to perform the act, using them as economically as possible, and not using the other muscles to perform movements which do not contribute to the act or which interfere with it. Expend constructively both the mental and physical energy (economical, neuromuscular, perceptive movement). In coordinated, graceful, and efficient movement, the opposing muscles must be relaxed and lengthen readily and easily."

8 Philip J. Rasch and Roger K. Burke, *Kinesiology and Applied Anatomy Sixth Edition* (Philadelphia: Lea & Febinger, 1978), p. 89.

9 Lee, *Tao of Jeet Kune Do*, p. 53.

10 Lee, ed. John Little, *Jeet Kune Do: Bruce Lee's Commentaries on the Martial Way*, p. 34.